Brussels in Focus
EC Access for Sport

by Bill Seary

in co-operation with the International Affairs Unit of the SPORTS COUNCIL

London, December 1992

Only

Foreword

During my eight years as a European Parliamentarian, I have witnessed the ever-increasing European Community involvement in almost all aspects of UK life. Sport is no exception to this. I am delighted, therefore, to welcome the publication of this much needed EC guide especially aimed at the needs of the sporting community. With 1993 and the Single Market upon us, the timely publication of this guide is in itself recognition of the interface between sport and the EC.

To maximise the potential EC benefit to sport and to ensure that Community sports initiatives are appropriately targeted, governing bodies of sport and other sports providers must know both what is happening in the Community and how to influence the European decision-making process.

The Sports Council, in co-operation with the British International Sports Committee, has to its credit recognised this. Sports bodies need not be in awe of the European Community. But for the European process to be effective we must all actively play our part. It is my hope that this practical and concise publication not only demystifies what happens in Brussels and Strasbourg, but is the first step towards UK sport itself influencing the European process and its cultural development.

John Tomlinson, MEP

Acknowledgements

This book could not have been written without the co-operation of many members of the sports community both in the UK and abroad. Special thanks must go to:

The governing bodies of sport in the UK for their help and ideas at the planning stage;

ENGSO EC Working Group members Bent Agerskov, Frederick Fallon, Marlis Rydzy-Gotz and Ger Wegener for their guidance and advice during the preparation phase;

British International Sports Committee members Eileen Gray and Charles Palmer for their encouragement and wise counsel throughout;

Those officers of the Commission of the European Communities and staff members of Technical Assistance Offices in Brussels for the patience and goodwill they have shown in answering our questions;

Christine Carroll and Marika Dimming, also in Brussels, who asked many questions on our behalf with tact and good humour;

Bridget Calvert and Wayne Day for editing and Aileen Earle for establishing the project and preparing Chapter 4, all from the Sports Council International Affairs Unit and BISC Secretariat.

Bill Seary

Iain Reddish

Contents

Contents

Introduction

Some eight months ago, a whole afternoon at the Sports Council's RecMan Conference was devoted to the European Community and Sport. That session highlighted both the lack of information and also the sense of confusion experienced by so many sports bodies concerning the EC and its effect on sport.

Since that meeting, the International Affairs Unit has faced a greatly increased flow of requests for information, advice and assistance on matters connected with Brussels. This guide is our attempt to service that need.

Our aim is to provide a context to the EC and a guide to its structures, to explain the main implications of Europe for sports organisations and to describe ways in which sport might make use of Community schemes. We have also included a chapter which describes Community support available for work with sports organisations in developing countries.

We hope that the guide will be of practical help to you when working with the European Community. It will be updated as the need arises. We would, therefore, be grateful for any corrections or ideas for additions or improvements.

Iain Reddish

Head of International Affairs,
Sports Council
Secretary,
British International Sports Committee

December 1992

Chapter (1)

Institutions of the European Community

There are three main Community institutions: the Commission, the Council of Ministers and the European Parliament.

The Commission

The most conspicuous of these institutions is **The Commission**. Narrowly defined, the Commission is the collective name for the seventeen men and women, currently presided over by Jacques Delors, who form the executive body of the Community. They are responsible for administering the programmes of the Community, for representing the Community to other countries, for proposing draft legislation and budgets and for policing the laws of the European Community. The Commission, more broadly defined, covers all the officers who work in support of the Commissioners. There are about 12 000 of these international civil servants. In addition each member of the Commission has a small personal staff, called his or her "cabinet".

The members of the Commission are appointed by the Council of Ministers (see below). In effect each of the smaller countries of the EC appoint one member and each of the larger members (Germany, Spain, France, Italy and the UK) appoints two. By tradition the countries that appoint two Commissioners arrange for them to come from different political tendencies. Thus there is normally one Conservative and one Labour Commissioner from the UK. At present the people involved are Sir Leon Brittan and Mr Bruce Millan respectively.

The staff of the Commission are organised in twenty-three "Directorates General", each identified by a Roman number. Thus the Directorate General dealing with Information, Communication and Culture (which includes sport) is number X – often referred to as "DG X". The work of the various Directorates General is co-ordinated by a Secretariat-General. (See Appendix 1 for complete list of Directorates-General.)

Council of Ministers

The **Council of Ministers** is the institution that takes the final decision on the Commission's proposals for European Community laws and programmes of action. The Council is composed of one minister from each country, the minister concerned varying with the topic under discussion. Some subjects need frequent meetings – the agriculture ministers, for example, meet almost every month. Other topics are dealt with less often or, in some cases, only on an ad hoc basis. Sports ministers, for instance, last met in Rome in December 1990.

The Council has its own secretariat, which also provides a base for other co-operation between the twelve which is outside the scope of the treaties. The work of the Council is steered by each country in turn for a six month term (see box opposite for a timetable). This term of office is called the "presidency". The presidency confers no extra influence on the outcome of discussions, but it does give considerable influence over which subjects are

discussed and which are left for the time being. The country holding the presidency also often represents the twelve community countries, for example at the United Nations or when making representations about, say, human rights issues to other governments. In some cases the presidency is supported by the country which has just done its turn and the country which is preparing to take over – this is called the "troika". The "extended troika" also involves the country before last and the country after next.

Presidencies 1993 - 1995

1993		**1995**	
January - June	Denmark	January - June	France
July - December	Belgium	July - December	Spain
1994			
January - June	Greece		
July - December	Germany		

UK Permanent Representative and COREPER

The work of the ministers is prepared by the "Permanent Representatives" of the various governments. In effect, these people are the ambassadors of the countries to the European Community. The office of the United Kingdom's representative is known as "UKREP". The Permanent Representatives meet on a body called **COREPER**. The preparation for their meetings, in turn, is done by a host of working groups involving the specialist members of the staff of the permanent representatives or, often, national civil servants who fly in for the meetings. The Council is in fact the legislature of the Community. None the less, Council, COREPER and working group meetings are held in private and the minutes are not published.

European Parliament

The last of the three main institutions, the **European Parliament** is composed of 518 elected MEPs. Eighty-one of these are elected from the United Kingdom (see Appendix 2 for full list). Elections are held every fifth year, the next one being due in 1994. MEPs sit in cross-national political groups. The British Labour MEPs sit with the Socialists and the Conservatives sit with the Christian Democrats. These are the two largest groups in the Parliament and dominate the proceedings. There are half a dozen smaller groups. The Parliament does much of its work in specialist Committees (see page 11 for a list of the Committees).

An MEP divides his or her working life between the full sessions of the Parliament (normally in Strasbourg), Committee meetings (normally in Brussels), political groups meetings (also Brussels) and, for UK MEPs, their constituency. MEPs also take part in "Intergroup" meetings. An intergroup is a multi-political, cross-national group of MEPs who come together to look after common concerns in a particular area. For sports organisations, the most important of these is the Intergroup on Sport, which is chaired by John Tomlinson, MEP for Birmingham West. Intergroups tend to meet in Strasbourg at the time of a plenary session.

Intergroups of MEPs

The Parliament's main task is the review of draft legislation proposed by the Commission before the Council decides whether or not to adopt it. Over recent years the Parliament has increased its influence over the final form of legislation. This is a process that is expected to continue, the Parliament being the only European Community institution with any degree of democratic accountability. Its powers at present include shared responsibility with the Council for the setting of the Community's annual budget, the power to question the Commission and the Council and (so far not used) the power to dismiss the Commission as a whole.

In addition to these three institutions, there is a wide range of other bodies with greater or lesser degrees of independence within the structures of the European Community.

European Court of Justice

The most important of these is the **European Court of Justice**, based in Luxembourg. The Court is completely independent from the other institutions in the decisions it makes. European Community laws and treaties are policed by the Commission but it is the European Court of Justice which has the authority to interpret legislation and make authoritative judgements.

Court of Auditors

Also fully independent is the **Court of Auditors**. The report of this body on each year's accounts is submitted first to the Council and then to the Parliament, which grants the Commission a "discharge" when it is satisfied that everything is in order. Both the Court and the Parliament have, in the past, pointed to weaknesses in the financial controls, leading to improvements.

CEDEFOP

The Community sponsors two organisations which function independently. The **European Foundation for the Improvement of Living and Working Conditions** looks at a wide range of issues. In recent years it has started to move away from being only concerned with employment-related matters. The **European Centre for the Development of Vocational Training** (known as CEDEFOP from its name in French) provides technical support on vocational training, equivalence of qualifications and related matters.

Economic and Social Committee

The Commission and the Council are supported by many advisory committees. Chief among these is the **Economic and Social Committee**. The role of this body in relation to legislation in its area is similar to that of the Parliament. Commission proposals come to it and are considered by the appropriate subject "section" (roughly equivalent to the Parliament's committee). The report of the section goes to a plenary meeting to form the basis of the Economic and Social Committee's opinion on the proposal. The members of

the Committee sit in three "groups", one of employers' representatives, one of trade union representatives and one of "other interests". This last group includes people with backgrounds in agriculture, academia, the voluntary sector and local authorities. Members of the Economic and Social Committee are nominated by their national governments for a four year term of office. The next renewal is due in 1994.

Technically outside the scope of the European Community, but closely linked to its work on harmonisation, are the sister organisations CEN (**Comité Européen de Normalisation**) and CENELEC (**Comité Européen de Normalisation Electrotechnique**). The members of these organisations are the national standards bodies of the countries of the European Economic Area (see Appendix 3). It is the job of CEN and CENELEC to develop European standards for goods. Chapter 4 refers to the implications for sports organisations of this work.

**CEN
CENELEC**

The Committees of the European Parliament

1	Foreign Affairs and Security
	SC1A Security and Disarmament
	SC1B Human Rights
2	Agriculture, Fisheries and Rural Development
	SC2 Fisheries
3	Budgets
4	Economic and Monetary Affairs and Industrial Policy
	SC4 Monetary Affairs
5	Energy, Research and Technology
6	External Economic Relations
7	Legal Affairs and Citizens' Rights
8	Social Affairs, Employment and the Working Environment
9	Regional Policy, Regional Planning and Relations with Regional and Local Authorities
10	Transport and Tourism
11	Environment, Public Health and Consumer Protection
12	Culture, Youth, Education and the Media
13	Development and Co-operation
14	Civil Liberties and Internal Affairs
15	Budgetary Control
16	Institutional Affairs
17	Rules of Procedure, Verification of Credentials and Immunities
18	Women's Rights
19	Petitions

NB: The "SC" numbers refer to sub-committees.

EEA
EFTA

A separate treaty establishes the **European Economic Area**. This brings the Community together with the **European Free Trade Area**. This treaty envisages the extension to the EFTA countries of the freedom of movement being established in the European Community.

For further information on the functions of the European Community see Appendix 4.

Chapter (2)

How decisions are made in the European Community

In theory the **decision-making process** in the European Community is simple. Proposals are made by the Commission. They go for comment to the European Parliament and, often, to the Economic and Social Committee. They then go to the Council, which decides whether or not to adopt them. In certain cases, the Parliament has a second chance to influence the decision. A flow chart of the process appears in Appendix 5.

Commission Proposal

The Commission's **formal Proposal**, however, is not really the beginning. The basic idea may, in fact, come from the Commission. It is quite likely these days to be part of a programme of legislation which has already been discussed by the Parliament and the Council. Many of the proposals in recent years, for example, were listed in a Commission document of 1985 which specified the legislation needed to guarantee freedom of movement of goods, services, people and capital. This document, often called the "White Paper", had almost 300 items.

Single Market "White Paper"

The Commission can face pressure from the Parliament or the Council to make proposals on particular matters. Indeed the original Treaty of Rome and some of the subsequent treaties amending it have placed a definite requirement on the Commission to make proposals on certain subjects.

Consultation process

Once the Commission has decided to draft a proposal, its staff comes under pressure about the contents from governments, MEPs and other interested groups such as the business community and non-governmental organisations. The Commission officials sometimes organise informal **consultation** meetings with such groups before submitting a draft proposal to the Commission.

Official Journal of the European Communities

After the Commission has agreed on a formal proposal, there is a short delay while the Commissioners' aides sort out any ambiguity and while the proposal is translated into the nine working languages of the Community. It then appears in the **Official Journal of the European Communities** and it is also issued, with an explanatory memorandum, as a Commission document. Commission documents, usually referred to as COM documents, are identified by a number of the form COM(YY)nn, where YY identifies the year and nn is a running number.

The proposal is then sent to the Council of Ministers where, normally, it goes to a working group (see page 9). At the same time copies are sent to the European Parliament and, if appropriate, to the Economic and Social Committee (see page 10).

European Parliament stage

In the Parliament it goes to the most appropriate committee which appoints a Rapporteur and a small group of MEPs to look at the text. The Rapporteur produces a draft opinion, commenting on the proposal and, often, suggesting amendments. This report is discussed and adopted by the Committee. The

proposal then goes to a "plenary" session, involving all the MEPs, which can make further amendments in adopting a formal opinion on the proposal. Before it goes to the plenary session, the Commission is asked whether it accepts the amendments that the Parliament is likely to adopt. Sometimes the Parliament is not satisfied with the Commission's reply and sends the proposal back to Committee, preventing the Council from concluding the process.

At the same time, and by a rather similar process involving the appropriate section, the Economic and Social Committee also produces an opinion on matters falling within its scope.

Consultation with Economic and Social Committee

What happens next depends upon the nature of the matter in hand. In the simplest case COREPER looks at the proposal, the result of the discussions in the Council's working group and the opinions of the Parliament and the Economic and Social Committee. It then prepares for a meeting of the Council of Ministers in one of two ways. Either it prepares a final text which the Council adopts without discussion or it identifies the key issues on which the various governments are still disagreeing. These are then discussed by the Ministers before they make a decision. Depending upon the subject under discussion and the nature of the decision being taken, the Council acts either by unanimity or by **"Qualified Majority"**.

COREPER and Council decision

The Qualified Majority

For a qualified majority decision, each Minister has a number of votes depending upon the size of his or her country. France, Germany, Italy and the UK get 10. Other countries get fewer, down to Luxembourg which gets 2. For a decision to be made, 54 out of the 76 votes have to be in favour, which means that no two countries can block the decision by themselves.

For questions relating to the freedoms of movement, services, goods and capital a more complicated system is used known as the **"Co-operation Procedure"** whereby Parliament has the chance to discuss proposals and, under certain circumstances, can actually make permanent changes.

Co-operation Procedure

When the decision has been taken, the text is translated into all the working languages and published in the Official Journal.

These stages, however, do not always complete the process. In many cases the legislation takes the form of a **Directive** (see Appendix 6 for a description of the various kinds of proposal). Directives need to be incorporated into national legislation and, typically, two years are allowed for this to take place.

Incorporation into national legislation

Procedure for agreeing the budget

The **budget** of the Community is decided by a separate procedure. The Commission seeks expenditure estimates from the other institutions and then produces the first draft budget which is submitted to the Council. This is normally done in the first half of the preceding year. The Council makes any amendments it deems necessary and then sends the budget to the Parliament. The Parliament can, if it sees fit, amend some of the items and suggest that the Council amends the others. The budget returns to the Council for a second reading for consideration, only, of the Parliament's amendments and suggestions. Finally it returns to the Parliament, which may reinstate some of its modifications and then, normally, adopts it.

It is, however, open to the Parliament, if there are important reasons, to reject the entire budget and ask the Commission to start the process again. If everything proceeds according to plan, the Parliament's adoption of the budget comes in mid-December, ready to be implemented from the 1st of January.

It is in implementation that the decisions of most interest to many readers are taken. As soon as it knows the figures for the budget, the Commission is in a position to finalise its plans for the year. It is at this stage that grant applications come up for consideration. The decision on each application is strictly a matter for the Commission though for some of the programmes it calls on the assistance of outside consultants or advisory committees. Further information about this is given in Chapter 5.

Chapter (3)

Lobbying in the European Community

Preparation for lobbying

In preparation for lobbying you must not only know the details of the specific issues of concern but also be in a position to show whoever you are dealing with that you have a fair idea of how the EC works. You are likely to be taken less seriously if it is clear that you have not bothered to find out how the Community functions. The box below gives ideas about who to approach for different issues.

Local contacts in the UK

Lobbying the European Community does not have to be a difficult or expensive process. In many cases influence can be brought to bear by making **local contact** and by the use of phone calls and correspondence.

Role of MPs

Such local contacts will include your **MP**, your MEP and your local authority. Your MP is important because he or she can raise your concern with national civil servants and with Ministers. These people are important in the work of the Council of Ministers (see opposite and also page 8).

Who should you be trying to influence?

1 *You want the Community to take action on something.*
The Commission is the key here, though national governments are also important influences. Another possibility is to petition the Parliament.

2 *The Commission has made a proposal which would adversely affect your sport.*
The Council will take the final decision. Influence it through the Parliament, the Economic and Social Committee, national governments or indeed the Commission itself which could withdraw or amend its proposal or, more realistically, react sympathetically to amendments suggested by the Parliament.

3 *Your rights under European Community law have been infringed.*
The ultimate judgement will be made by the Court of Justice but you will probably have to take your case through national courts in the first instance. Alternatively, raise the matter with the Commission. They may be willing to take up your case. One other possibility would be to petition the Parliament.

4 *You think the organisation of a programme – or a grant scheme – is unhelpful.*
You should approach the Commission. They have quite a lot of discretion in many of these schemes. More radical change will be equivalent to a new proposal (see the first paragraph in this box).

5 *You have applied to the Commission for a grant and want to make sure you have the best chance of being successful.*
Considerable care is needed here. Decisions on individual grants are normally the prerogative of the Commission and the relevant staff can react badly to being unreasonably pestered. See Chapter 5 for advice.

MEPs are important because of their role in forming the budget of the European Community and because of their increasing influence in the framing of legislation. They also have access to up-to-date information about what is happening and what is being planned; they can use their transnational links to identify people in other countries who share your concern; and as elected representatives they are often anxious to be helpful. Frequently the help will be in the form of putting you in touch with another MEP of the same party who sits on the relevant committee.

Help from MEPs

National organisations will probably want to go direct to the MEPs on the appropriate committee. Their details are in a directory available free from the London Office of the Parliament (2 Queen Anne's Gate, London SW1H 9AA, Tel: 071 222 0411, Fax: 071 222 2713) and a list of UK MEPs is given in Appendix 2.

Local authorities are valuable sources of information on European Community matters. All counties and many districts now have specialist staff working on European Community questions. These people are the key to some funding (see European Regional Development Fund page 58). They are also knowledgeable about many policy matters. At national level they are supported by the Local Government International Bureau (LGIB) (35 Great Smith Street, London SW1P 3BJ, Tel: 071 222 1636, Fax: 071 233 2179). The LGIB supports the UK members of a consultative group established for local authorities by the Commission. This gives them particular insight into, and some influence on, the policy-making process.

Local authorities

Local Government International Bureau

The **UK civil servants** who serve on Council working groups (see page 9) are key contacts. They know the latest Commission thinking and they know the position of other countries. Very often they will be prepared to discuss these with you. They also contribute to advice to Ministers, so it is important that they are aware of your position.

Whitehall

The civil servants based at the UK representation in Brussels **(UKREP)** are also useful contacts. They know the position of other governments as well as our own and it is normally easy to locate the relevant person, which is not always the case in London. For any major changes in approach, however, it will be necessary to mobilise politicians and particularly the relevant Ministers.

Both Houses of Parliament in **Westminster** have **Select Committees** looking into proposed European Community legislation. The **Lords Committee** is particularly important. It has sub-committees which look at a selection of EC proposals in detail. Their reports are debated in the main House and can be an important influence on the line the government takes at the Council of Ministers. Details about current members of the Select Committee and its sub-committee are available from the Clerk to the European Community

Westminster procedures

Committee (House of Lords, London SW1A 0PW, Tel: 071 219 6412). For the Commons Committee, contact the Clerk to the Select Committee on European Legislation (House of Commons, London SW1A 0AA, Tel: 071 291 5467).

EC Commission London Office

The **London Office of the Commission** (8 Storey's Gate, London SW1P 3AT, Tel: 071 973 1992, Fax: 071 973 1900/1910) should be kept informed. They offer a Citizens' Europe Advisory Service to people who want advice on their rights in the new Europe – ring between 2pm and 5pm on a Monday afternoon. You should also contact any members of the Economic and Social Committee who might be interested. There is a list of them in Vacher's European Companion (see page 78).

Contact with Brussels

Brussels is the focal point for contact with the people who influence decisions in the European Community. It is the main base of the Commission, it is the home of the Economic and Social Committee and it is in Brussels that the European Parliament's committees and political groups (see page 9) meet. In addition, although the members of the Council are best influenced in their national capitals, Brussels is one of the main meeting places for groups who want to co-ordinate national lobbying to ensure that it has maximum impact on the Council.

Contact by post

Contact with Brussels does not need to be in person. It is best to try to **contact both officials and MEPs by post in the first place**. A short statement of the issue that you feel needs attention and of what you want that particular person to do can be very effective. If you are lobbying for change to a Commission proposal, try to be as positive as you can. "Yes but ..." will normally get better results than "That's nonsense". You should look at your statement anew for each approach. The interests of the various parts of the system are different and it is important to tailor your approach to respect this. Do not be afraid to write in English. Virtually all the people you contact will be able to read it and those who cannot will find it easy to find a translator for good English.

Such letters should be sent:
- to the official who seems most appropriate (Vacher's European Companion can help here, so too can the London Office of the Commission);
- to MEPs – select them from the relevant committee or intergroup and from different parties; and
- probably to three Commissioners – the one under whose remit the matter falls and the two who come from the United Kingdom.

Follow up by telephone

You will probably need to follow these letters with telephone calls. You are likely to find that Commission officials are very willing to talk to anyone with a serious issue to raise, though there may be a certain amount of passing you from department to department if you are raising something which has not previously been recognised as an EC issue. The Commission is a relatively open bureaucracy, much more so, in fact, than Whitehall. It is cautious about organisations with commercial interests, but if it is happy about your non-profit motives and interested in your approach it can be very co-operative. Some organisations have found themselves actually drafting proposals for the Commission to adopt.

MEPs themselves can sometimes be somewhat difficult to contact but their assistants in either Brussels or at their home base are often well informed and helpful. The Parliament will also accept petitions from European Community citizens. Send them to your MEP or to the Chair of the Petitions Committee (European Parliament, 97-113 Rue Belliard, 1040 Brussels, Belgium).

You may get all you need from correspondence and telephone calls. If you do decide that face to face meetings are necessary you should first remember that officials are more often away "on mission" than their UK counterparts. This has two implications. On the one hand it means that you need to plan a visit carefully to make sure that you see the important people. On the other hand it means that the officials may well be somewhere near you in the not too distant future. Getting them to come to you is cheaper, and it may have more impact if you can show them your work.

Personal visits to Brussels

If possible, time a visit to Brussels to coincide with a meeting of the appropriate committee of the Parliament. These are often open to the public and can be informative. They also greatly increase your chances of meeting interested MEPs, not just from the UK. When planning a programme of visits, the ideal is to set up the main appointments so that they are well spaced. This then allows you to follow up immediately any suggestions, possibly about other people to see. It also gives you a better chance of writing up your notes quickly. This can be a vital aid to your memory in later stages.

European Parliament in Strasbourg

A visit to Strasbourg can also be useful because it is at the monthly plenary sessions of the **Parliament in Strasbourg** that all the MEPs come together. It provides an opportunity to make yourself known to them and the many other people who gather in Strasbourg for the week. Many intergroup meetings take place during the week of plenary session. Serious lobbying of the Parliament, however, has to start in the Brussels committees.

Importance of pan-European activity

One major key to exerting influence on Council decisions is to create favourable climates in as many national capitals as possible. The government holding the presidency is particularly important because of its influence over the agendas of Council meetings. In fact you should concentrate on the country which will be taking over the presidency, as governments plan their programmes for the presidency well in advance.

In any controversial case you will need to find partners in other countries. Sports organisations are well served with international networks, based on years of international competition. These networks will need to be exploited to the full. The first step in this must be to ascertain the interests and perceptions of your partner organisations. They are bound to differ from yours in detail, and they may differ in basics. You should always, however, be able to find a common platform that you will all be able to support and which has much more chance of impressing not only the Council, but also Commission officials.

There are no magic formulas for successful lobbying in the European Community. Chapter 5 deals with the question of getting money from the European Community.

Chapter (4)

EC issues affecting sports organisations

EC sports policy

In 'The European Community and Sport', published in 1991, the Commission clearly pledged itself to "show proper regard for the principle of subsidiarity (see Appendix 4) both to the official authorities and to the organizations responsible for sport". However, its first priority is to the establishment of a single market. Sport is estimated to account for 1% of the Community's GNP and cannot avoid being involved as an economic activity. When it can be defined as an economic activity, sport is subject to all the legal and institutional imperatives of the Community (see box below). This includes all legislation designed to remove protectionist barriers. This legislation is considered in the following sections.

Walrave and Koch v. Union Cycliste Internationale

In 1973 the International Cycling Association established new regulations for the World Championship of the motor-pacing event, which determined that the motorcyclist and the cyclist should have the same nationality. In 1974 two Dutch motorcyclists, Walrave and Koch, who wanted to ride with, respectively, a Belgian and a German cyclist, appealed against the regulations on the ground that they contravened articles 7, 48 and 59 of the Treaty of Rome. The Court of Justice was asked for an opinion and ruled that "The practice of sport is subject to Community law only in so far as it constitutes an economic activity within the meaning of Article 2 of the Treaty."

The Court also said that prohibition of discrimination which interferes with the freedom of a national of a member state to provide services, to establish him or herself, or to take up work in another Member State "does not affect the composition of sports teams, in particular of national teams, since the composition of these teams is a question concerning matters of sporting interest only, and thus unrelated to economic activity."

However, it left to the national court the question of whether the pacer was a member of the national team and, therefore, not within the scope of the relevant European Community law, or an employee who would, therefore, be subject to EC discrimination law.

Sport as an economic activity

It is tempting to try to determine what constitutes an economic activity by reference to concepts of **amateur and professional sport**, especially as the European Court of Justice referred to these definitions in the case of **Dona v. Mantero** (box opposite). The statement that only professional and semi-professional sport comes under the umbrella of EC legislation is, however, too simplistic. In the first instance there is no definition of the terms "amateur" and "professional" in the **Treaty of Rome** (see Appendix 4). Secondly, the definitions held in the sporting world, which vary greatly in any case, bear little relation to the European Community's interest in whether a person or body involved in sport is participating in "economic activities which have the character of gainful employment or remunerated services".

Individuals considered to be pursuing an economic activity, whether as athlete, instructor, guide or sports manager are protected by all the relevant EC legislation, in particular in the area of free movement and non-discrimination on the basis of nationality.

Dona v. Mantero

Mr Dona was asked by Mr Mantero, the former Chairman of the Rovigo Football Club, to head-hunt players for the team. He published an advertisement in a Belgian newspaper to this end. Mr Mantero refused to pay him for costs incurred, referring to the Rules of the Italian Football Federation, according to which only players affiliated to that federation may take part in matches, membership being in principle only open to players of Italian nationality.

In 1976 the case was referred to the European Court of Justice who ruled that: "Rules or a national practice, even adopted by a sporting organization, which limit the right to take part in football matches as professional or semi-professional players solely to the nationals of the State in question, are incompatible with Article 7 and, as the case may be, with Articles 48 to 51 or 59 to 66 of the Treaty unless such rules or practice exclude foreign players from participation in certain matches for reasons which are not of an economic nature, which relate to the particular nature and context of such matches and are thus of sporting interest only. It is for the national court to determine the nature of the activities submitted to its judgment and to take into account Articles 7, 48 and 59 of the Treaty, which are mandatory in nature, in order to judge the validity or the effects of a provision inserted into the rules of a sporting organization."

In other words, professional or semi-professional football players from other Member States may only be excluded from playing for purely sporting interests, for example for national teams competing in international competitions. Otherwise, association rules excluding such players may infringe Community legislation on free movement of workers. National courts are to determine what constitutes sporting interests as opposed to economic interests.

Free movement of individuals

The Treaty of Rome guarantees the freedom for every EC citizen to work, to seek work, to set up business or to provide services in any EC Member State. Community citizens may not be discriminated against on grounds of nationality. This applies both to employees and to self-employed people. People working in sport are guaranteed the same rights as all other workers.

However, in two cases (see **Walrave & Koch v. Union Cycliste Internationale** box opposite and **Dona v. Mantero** box above) the European Court of Justice made an exception in the case of **the composition of national teams**, "the formulation of which is a question of purely sporting interest and as such has nothing to do with economic activity". Further, the impact of Community law on the selection even of professional teams at the local level is far from clear.

UEFA agreement

On 17th April 1991, Commission Vice President, Martin Bangemann, responsible for internal market matters, reached a **"gentlemen's agreement" with UEFA** (Union of European Football Associations). According to this agreement, as from the 1992-93 season, national associations under the umbrella of UEFA can limit the number of foreign players in the line-up for domestic first division matches. They do not have to allow in their teams more than three non-nationals and two assimilated players (non-nationals who have been playing without interruption in the country concerned for five years). The legality of this is under question (see box below) and the Commission has stated that it is examining the UEFA rules and regulations with a view to possible proceedings under competition rules. In the meantime, while it is not essential for governing bodies of sport to alter their rules and regulations, they should monitor EC developments and be ready to take the necessary action to ensure that their regulations do not contravene ultimately agreed EC legislation.

The UEFA Agreement

An action challenging the legality of the UEFA agreement was brought against the Commission by Jean-Marc Bosman, a professional football player from Belgium. The Court of Justice dismissed the action, declaring it inadmissible as the agreement was not a legally binding act and therefore was not under its jurisdiction.

So in July 1992, Bosman brought another action against UEFA and the Royal Football Club de Liege before a Belgian court. This court referred the matter to the European Court of Justice requesting its advice on whether the UEFA rules are compatible with EC law, and in particular with the provisions relating to free movement and competition. We are still awaiting their opinion.

The European Parliament for its part denounced the practices restricting the free circulation of professional sportsmen and women within the Community in a Resolution of April 1989. In its plenary session in November 1991 it again reaffirmed its opposition to the agreement on the current transfer system and to any other restrictions to the free movement of professional footballers in the EC.

Equivalence of qualifications

For there to be true freedom of movement of EC citizens, each country must recognise **qualifications** gained in other European Community countries. **Union Nationale des Entraineurs v. Heylens** (see box opposite) gives an example where this was at stake. The Community noted this problem at an early stage and decided to tackle it profession by profession. Its approach was to compare the education and training required by each Member State for a given profession and, as far as possible, to harmonise it. So far a number of sectoral Directives have been agreed (for doctors, dentists and architects for example). This approach, however, proved difficult and slow. The Architects' Directive took 17 years to agree.

> **Union Nationale des Entraineurs v. Heylens**
>
> In 1986, M Heylens, a Belgian national holding a Belgian football coaching qualification, wished to coach a French team. However, the French authorities insisted on a French qualification. M Heylens continued to coach his French team and was subject to criminal proceedings in the French courts. The court asked for a preliminary ruling from the European Court of Justice (ECJ) in Luxembourg. Such rulings are binding on Member States.
>
> The ECJ held that any decision refusing permission to work as a coach should be based on stated reasons which could be justified under the Treaty, and should be subject to a process of appeal in which its legality under EC law could be tested. The implication was that unless good reasons could be given, such as substantial differences in qualifications, a refusal of this sort would be contrary to the Treaty of Rome.

First employment directive

In 1985, therefore, the Commission suggested a major new approach to tackle the remaining restrictions by proposing a new directive. The **'Directive on a General System for the Recognition of Higher Education Diplomas** awarded on completion of professional education and training of at least three years' duration' was adopted by the Council in 1988. It applies to all professions to which access is in some way restricted by the State and which require at least three years' university level education or equivalent plus any appropriate job-based training. It is therefore of little relevance to the sports sector. The professions regulated in the United Kingdom for the purposes of this directive include school teachers, physiotherapists and psychologists.

Second directive on diplomas

The Community has now moved on to adopt the **'Directive on a Second General System for Mutual Recognition of Qualifications'**. The scope of this directive, which must be implemented by 18th June 1994, covers higher or post-secondary level diplomas gained after a period of less than three years and secondary education diplomas. It will apply to certain categories of people who have not obtained qualifications but who have professional experience. The Directive specifically takes account of the UK's system of National Vocational Qualifications. Areas which might well be affected by this legislation include coach education and recreation management.

Recognition of qualifications

The directive distinguishes between diplomas and certificates. Diploma courses can be defined as post-secondary courses of at least one year's duration; certificates refer to post-secondary courses of under one year. The procedures for **mutual recognition of training** are very complex as they cover situations where both the host and the original State require equivalent qualifications and where one State might require a professional diploma whilst another State requires only a certificate. Every case has to be carefully considered. In some instances the host Member State may require the applicant to provide evidence of professional experience, to complete an adaptation period not exceeding three years (or two years in the case of a certificate) or to take an aptitude test.

The single market for services

The single market will ensure that services are available equally in all Member States (see box below).

Distribution of Barcelona Olympic Games Tickets

Traditionally the Organising Committee of the Olympic Games calls for every National Olympic Committee to nominate a single ticket agency in their country to distribute the tickets. That agency is only permitted to sell tickets within the country and it can only sell to nationals of the country.

The Commission of the European Communities challenged this arrangement as it was deemed to contravene EC competition law. The distribution system in Europe had to be amended as a result of this so that EC citizens were free to purchase tickets in any one of the 12 member states.

Similar problems have arisen in the case of the ticket distribution system for the All England Lawn Tennis Club (for Wimbledon).

Protection of the consumer

The service sector, which dominates the EC economy, is extremely important as regards consumer safety. Under article 100 (a) of the Treaty of Rome the Commission envisages a high level of protection for the consumer. Although there is a positive trend in favour of persons injured by defective services, there are wide variations within the Community in the level of protection a consumer receives. Some of these differences relate to the burden of proof. At present in the UK the consumer facing difficulties has to prove that the provider of the service was at fault.

Liability of service suppliers

The proposed Council **Directive on the Liability of Suppliers of Services** seeks to establish the reverse burden of proof so that it is the service provider who has to prove that they were not negligent in the provision of the service. In this proposal the definition of "service" is wide enough to cover all kinds of services, including all those offered in the sporting world. It is important to note that this directive also applies to services provided free of charge.

If it is adopted in its present form, this directive could have significant implications for all sports coaches and leaders, as well as life savers and mountain rescue teams. At the time of writing, the proposal was being examined by the European Parliament's Committee on Legal Affairs and Citizens' Rights.

Public procurement procedures

The opening of European Community **public procurement procedures** is one of the many aspects of the opening of the European Community internal market. Public purchasing represents 15% of Community domestic product.

National and local governments have traditionally favoured domestic suppliers of goods and services, a practice which is not compatible with a single European market.

A plethora of directives concerning the opening of procurement markets has been adopted covering public supplies contracts, public works contracts and public services contracts over a certain value and setting common procedures for public procurement. These include rules on contract award procedures, technical specifications, advertising and statistical reporting.

We can therefore expect some local authority recreation facilities to be built by contractors from outside the UK. Other contracts for the supply of services within the sports sector may also be won by companies from other Member States.

One further aspect of the freedom of movement of services concerns **gambling – and lotteries** in particular. A report on 'Gambling in the Single Market – a Study of the Current Legal and Market Situation' was published by the Commission at the end of 1991. The Commission is now examining this issue with a view to possible legislation. There are two main concerns about the prospect of the harmonisation of gambling legislation. The first is that ticket sales from non-national lotteries will benefit other Member States. The second is that the high level of revenue for sport and the arts which accrues from lotteries (such as the Foundation for Sport and the Arts fund by the football pools and the proposed national lottery) will be threatened by less charitable competitors from other Member States.

Harmonisation of lotteries

Already a case challenging the closed market in lotteries has been referred to the European Court of Justice (see box below).

Cross-Border Sales of Lottery Tickets

In July 1992 the English High Court of Justice asked the European Court of Justice for a ruling in a case between H.M. Customs and Excise and 1. Gerhart Schindler and 2. Jörg Schindler regarding publicity material for a lottery. The Schindlers of Germany wanted to sell lottery tickets within the UK but their mail was impounded by H.M. Customs and Excise under UK gambling law. The European Court of Justice is to determine whether or not European Community law will apply or whether gambling is subject to Member State regulations on law and social order, ie. whether subsidiarity applies. The case will not be completed until the end of 1993 or 1994 and until a decision is reached the position on lotteries is inconclusive.

Member State governments wish to maintain regulations whereas the commercial lottery operators are seeking total liberalisation.

The free movement of goods

Harmonisation of technical standards

In May 1985, the European Community Ministers agreed on a **'New Approach to Technical Harmonisation and Standards'** to achieve the free movement of goods. "New Approach" directives set out in general terms the essential requirements for health, safety and the environment, which must be met before products may be sold in the United Kingdom or anywhere else in the Community. Products meeting the essential requirements bear the symbol of the European Committee.

The work of CEN

An important "New Approach" directive (the Personal Protective Equipment Directive) came into force on 1 July 1992. It sets out the essential safety requirements for **personal protective equipment**. These standards are also being considered by the **Comité Européen de Normalisation** (see page 11). CEN has recently studied the standards needed to assure the highest practicable level of safety with regard to operational requirements, convenience and economics in a number of sports (see box below).

Sports and CEN

Inter-governmental bodies have endorsed the value of international standards as the basis of regulations designed to overcome trade barriers within the Community from January 1993. Since 1961 the production of European standards has been undertaken by CEN and it now has over 200 technical committees looking at the harmonisation of product standards.

The development of European standards for sports and other recreational equipment is a comparatively new area of work. Work on sports equipment is being undertaken by CEN Technical Committee 136 and its various working groups. Consultation stage has been reached on goals for football, handball and hockey. National associations and manufacturers have been given the opportunity to comment. Standards are currently being developed for volleyball, basketball, tennis and badminton. Again sports bodies are being consulted.

Work is also being undertaken concerned with gymnastic equipment and matting. Whilst there is clear agreement on the types of equipment and matting to be harmonised there has been some difficulty because of the different interpretation of the word gymnastics.

Other working groups are looking at stationary training equipment (ie. fitness and exercise equipment) and specialist equipment in the field of air, water and countryside sports including mountaineering equipment, paragliding equipment and diving accessories for skin divers.

Governing bodies with queries on these standards may contact Robin Barron at the Sports Council, Coronet House, Queens Street, Leeds LS1 4TW, Tel: 0532 436443, Fax: 0532 422189.

Other CEN Technical Committees also include work for sport, for example the Committee working on artificial surfaces including sports surfaces.

Fiscal frontiers prevent free movement of goods. After years of debate, the European Community is coming to a workable agreement on VAT. From 1st January 1993 to 1st January 1997 a transitional regime will be set in place. Under this regime, cross-frontier sales will be taxed in the country of destination of the goods. As from 1997 sales will be taxed in the country of origin.

Harmonisation of taxation including VAT

A minimum rate of 15% will apply across the European Community. There are, of course, exceptions and cases where **reduced rates** apply. It is proposed that admission to sporting events and the use of sports facilities should be subject to reduced rates at the discretion of individual States.

The ways in which particular sports are affected by the various European Community laws, practices and proposals are many and various (for examples see boxes below and on page 32). The remainder of this section deals with some of the issues of more general interest.

Examples of how sport is affected by the EC

Sponsorship, although not in itself subject to Community law, can often be seen as part of the promotion or marketing activity of the sponsoring company. Two main articles of the Treaty of Rome establish the rules on competition. Article 85 automatically renders null and void all agreements between undertakings which affect trade between Member States and distort competition in the single market. Article 86 prohibits an undertaking from abusing its dominant position. The Commission has begun to examine the question of sponsorship. It therefore becomes important that any sponsorship agreement is carefully drawn up so as to "offer a window of opportunity" to other suppliers.

Sponsorship

Exclusive **broadcasting rights** could be seen to be working against free competition. However, the case law of the Commission and the European Court of Justice makes it clear that the fact that a licensee has an exclusive licence and is not allowed to transmit outside, say, the UK nor to sub-license is not necessarily a problem. The court has ruled that in view of the characteristics of the industry, an exclusive exhibition licence is not in itself such as to prevent, restrict or distort competition. The Commission is contracting for a study in the field of exclusive broadcasting rights, which should address some of the issues relevant to sport.

Broadcasting rights

Firearms

The main provision of interest to sport in the 'Directive on the acquisition and possession of weapons" is the introduction of the "European Firearms Pass" for the purpose of taking part in target shooting in other Member States. The directive does not affect the application of national provisions concerning the carrying of weapons, hunting or target shooting.

Transport of Animals

Directive 90/425/EEC concerns veterinary checks applicable in intra-community trade in certain live animals. This includes most animals except small game, dogs and cats. The Directive abolished intra-EC border checks on live animals and replaces them with stricter inspections on the point of departure and random checks at the point of arrival.

Directive 90/426/EEC concerns animal health conditions governing equestrian movement and importation from third countries. This includes race-horses and showjumpers. Member States may not prohibit the movement of horses either within or across their borders to another Member State if they do not show any clinical sign of disease at inspection carried out during the 48 hours prior to their embarkation.

Directive 90/427/EEC concerns zootechnical and genealogical conditions governing equestrian intra-Community trade. Horses registered in the exporting Member State must be entered in the appropriate studbook of the Member State of destination.

Directive 90/428/EEC concerns equestrian trade intended for competition and lays down the conditions for participation therein.

The Commission was also expected to issue a proposal before the end of 1992 which would seek to protect the welfare of animals during transportation. Whilst the proposal would be aimed more specifically at farm animals, it was expected that horses would be included.

Boats

The Commission has published a proposal for a Council Directive on the approximation of laws, regulations and administrative provisions of the Member States regarding recreational craft. The directive would apply to recreational boats with a minimum length of 2.5 metres up to 24 metres, regardless of methods of propulsion. The directive would not apply to boats solely for racing (canoes, kayaks, surfboards, etc) or to boats with a crew and carrying passengers for commercial purposes.

The proposed directive deals with standards relating to risks entailed in using the craft such as falling overboard; structure, stability, buoyancy; and rescue, towing and mooring. It also outlines essential requirements for performance, fire protection, lights, and safety of the propulsion, fuel, electrical and steering systems.

The Commission recently undertook a study on exhaust gas regulation for pleasure boat propulsion engines, particularly concerned with the pollution of Lake Constance. It is believed that a directive in this area was not seen as a priority by DGXI (Environment), and that as far as the internal market was concerned the Commission could not accept industry's view that a directive was needed.

Minibus drivers are affected by a directive which has been adopted for the purpose of establishing mutual recognition of driving licences issued by Member States. **Minibuses** are classed with Public Service Vehicles but the directive allows Member States to authorise the driving in their territory of: "vehicles of Category D1 (maximum 16 seats in addition to the driver's seat and maximum authorized mass of 3500 kgs...) by holders over 21 years old of a driving licence for category B which was obtained at least 2 years before, provided that the vehicles are being used by non-commercial bodies for social purposes and that the driver provides his services on a voluntary basis".

Licensing regulations for minibuses

Fundraising and other direct mail activities would be affected by a **proposal on data protection** which was put forward by the Commission on 13th September 1990. The draft directive is intended to protect individuals from junk mail. It does so by requiring marketing concerns to obtain the consent of the individual to every new use of data held on them. The provisions are so severe that many organisations might be prevented from carrying out their current mailings. However, in response to a written question to the European Parliament, Commission Vice President Bangemann stated that the Commission recognised the special nature of non-profit-making associations. It is proposed that files held by such bodies relating to their members and correspondents would not be subject to the full application of the directive.

Data protection and direct mailing

The EC is playing an ever more important role in **the environment**, with consequences for most **countryside and water sports** and for motor sports.

Sport and the environment

The Council Directive on the Conservation of Natural Habitats and Wild Fauna and Flora was adopted in January 1992. It will designate special areas of conservation to form a European ecological network called Natura 2000. Once a site has been adopted the Member State concerned must designate it within six years and establish priorities for its maintenance or restoration.

In its March 1992 session, the European Parliament adopted a resolution on the Olympic Games in Albertville and the ecological damage they brought in their wake. The main criticism was that the Games and the preparations for them, which included building new roads and creating new ski slopes, caused intolerable environmental damage. The Commission called for financiers of future Winter Olympic Games to insist that an environmental impact assessment be carried out.

The Olympic Games and ecological damage

At the end of March 1992 the Commission adopted the fifth environmental action plan, due to run from 1993-2000. The main strategy behind the action programme is based on the realisation that environmental damage will never be prevented unless behavioural patterns of producers and consumers, governments and citizens alter to take the environment more into account.

It is still not clear exactly what impact these directives will have on sport, but sports organisations should ensure that they are fully aware of the impact of their sport on the environment and that they include an element of environmental education in their training.

Doping control

Criminal justice matters and, in particular, sports offences, drug-related or not, are outside the scope of the European Community. However, on 12th February 1992 the Commission adopted a **Code of Conduct in Doping**, which was first distributed at Albertville.

Furthermore, on 13th May 1992 the European Parliament adopted a Resolution on the subject of education for health and abuse of drugs in the Member States of the European Community and the Council of Europe. This Resolution referred to doping in sport:

"4.1 As far as penalties are concerned, affirms that:
- the complex range of different penalties for dope use currently applied by national and international sports federations must be further simplified, and standardised as far as possible, both between countries and between different sports;
- international and inter-federal co-operation and standardisation should ensure equal treatment on doping controls and penalties for athletes in different sports;"

It should be stressed that this Resolution is not binding, but it reflects the European Parliament's position on doping and sport.

Chapter **5**

Applying for grants from the European Community

The following five chapters describe some of the **grants** available from the European Community. You will find information about why the scheme was established, how it has been used or could be used by sports organisations and some idea of how much money is available and the contact information you need if you are going to proceed. In some cases you will also find a case study of a successful application.

The Community was conceived as, and to a large extent remains, an economic entity. Its activities are directed to economic aims which, in the Treaty of Rome, are described in terms of agriculture, transport, competition, co-ordinated economic policies, working conditions and the free movement of goods, services, capital and labour. The Community's powers outside these areas are tightly restricted.

Subsidiarity

Requirement for schemes to involve more than one country

In general the Community is also restricted to acting only when it can be more effective than national governments acting alone. This is the crux of the **"principle of subsidiarity"** (see Appendix 4) which has been much promoted. This restriction on the freedom of action of the Community means that grant programmes are often only open to projects which have a **"European dimension"**. The exact interpretation given to this phrase varies from scheme to scheme but, in almost all cases, it implies that at least two countries are involved (in many cases the minimum requirement is more than two) and that the organisers can show that they have thought about the impact of the Community on their work or vice-versa.

Another acknowledged role for the Community is in the **furthering of good practice**. In grant schemes this is sometimes reflected in a requirement that projects should be "innovative". Again, this word has a range of meanings. Sometimes, for example, it can mean "not attempted in any EC country". On other occasions there is active encouragement for schemes that are new in one country, but based on an idea that has been tried somewhere else in the Community. In almost all cases, it will pay to have some way of showing that what you are doing would be relevant in other EC countries.

Key policies of the EC

The European Community has a number of **key policies** which have influence throughout its work. Addressing one of these will almost always increase your chances of being considered seriously. Examples of this include the concern that the peripheral regions of the Community should take a full part in EC programmes, the interest in the position of people who move about the Community, the firm intention to see that men and women have **equal opportunities** in the world of work and, increasingly, the concern that people with disabilities can make full use of their talents and skills.

Languages of the Commission

The Community's programmes are administered by the Commission. The officials who do this work face constraints on their activities. **Language** is a

case in point. Eurocrats come from all European Community countries so there is no guarantee that your application will be dealt with by someone whose mother tongue is English. In fact people from the United Kingdom are exceptionally lucky; there are rather few Commission officials who have no English and many who are highly competent in our language. If you do not speak French, which is even more widespread, and you find yourself trying to talk to one of the few who have no English, do not despair. He or she will have a colleague nearby who can speak English and either deal with your query or act as an informal interpreter.

More important than language is the matter of background knowledge. You should bear in mind that the people you are writing for, or speaking to, are not necessarily well informed about the particular characteristics of your district, nor can you expect them to know in detail about the legislative or administrative situation in the UK. Appropriate brief and clear **explanatory material** is always helpful.

Information needed by the Commission

Another major constraint upon the work of the Commission is the **level of resources** available to it. This applies to the budget allocations. These are often minute in comparison with the demand. In an extreme case, one of the schemes could only accept 5% of the applications it received in 1991 before it ran out of money.

Financial resources of the EC

Resource limitations also apply to staff levels. The size of the Commission staff has been tightly controlled for many years now, while the work has continued to increase. Many of the smaller grant schemes are in effect controlled by one official who is also trying to do several other tasks at the same time. At times this means that the Commission has to resort to bureaucratic techniques to ensure that the work gets done, which can make the process seem somewhat haphazard to the applicant. It means, too, that applications that are clear and short, while providing all the information needed, are easier to deal with and are likely to be looked at more quickly.

Another problem, partly caused by lack of resources, is the delay that often occurs between your completing your side of the agreement and the money arriving in your bank account. With any substantial grant you should always enquire carefully about the expected payments schedule and allow an extra fortnight minimum for transfers. Even then, you should not rely upon the dates given as delays can occur at any stage. In general, grant applications to the European Community are characterised by short periods of intense activity while you try to get the forms in by the Commission's deadline, followed by long periods of apparent inactivity on its part.

Timescale for receipt of grant

Increasingly the Commission is resorting to farming the administration of programmes out either to "national co-ordinators" (the PETRA programme for

Co-ordination of grant applications

example – see page 51) or to contractors who establish a separate office for the purpose. This can be called an **"office for technical assistance"** or **"bureau d'assistance technique"** in French. This means, by way of an example, that enquiries about the FORCE programme (see page 50) are dealt with by the "BAT FORCE". In some cases, FORCE and PETRA both being examples, there are both national co-ordinators and a technical assistance office.

One of the administrative headaches that Commission officials face when dealing with the United Kingdom is the variety of financial years we have. Rather few UK organisations use financial years which co-incide with the calendar year, as would be standard practice elsewhere in Europe.

Projects covering more than one financial year

Few Commission grants are made on a multi-annual basis. Many allow a short extension into the following year but if your project straddles the 1st January you may have to make two applications, with no guarantee that the second will get the same decision as the first. A few years ago this lack of continuity was a major problem with the European Social Fund (see page 48) where many courses were based on the academic year and had to take the risk of starting before they knew whether the second part of the course would be supported.

Use of the ECU

The European Community uses the ecu for its financial arrangements. Often the grant you are offered will be specified in terms of ecus. Occasionally you will have to submit estimates expressed in them. At the time of writing each pound sterling is worth about 1.25 ecu. You will find that this rate is printed in all the quality newspapers.

Conditions of grant

Some of the grant schemes have requirements about **matching funds**. That is to say that the Commission will only pay up to a certain percentage of the total cost. With others there is no formal requirement for matching, but it is very rare for the Commission to be the only source of income. Not only are their resources limited, they are also aware that it is difficult for them to know how relevant a project is and how well it is likely to be managed by the applicants. They feel more secure if a local funder is also involved. With the **Structural Funds** (see box opposite and page 40 for eligible areas in the UK) and some other schemes the matching funds need to come from public funds. In all cases, having national or local government support can only help your application.

The range in size of the grants is enormous. Non-governmental organisations in the United Kingdom have received grants from one or two thousand up to millions of pounds. The really large sums come from the Structural Funds. Other grant schemes may offer only one-off grants of up to about £10 000.

Some of the larger grant programmes, especially in the research field, use a kind of **tendering procedure**. The "call for tender" is published in the Official Journal (see page 74) giving outline details and normally an address for further

The European Structural Funds – Basic Information

The European Structural Funds are so called because, by their size and their design, they are expected to make an improvement to the economic structures of the European Community. At present, the three funds are:-

- the European Social Fund – ESF (see page 48)
- the European Regional Development Fund – ERDF (see page 58) and
- the European Agricultural Guidance and Guarantee Fund – EAGGF – also known as FEOGA from the French title.

The three current structural funds have diverse origins and histories. Over the last ten years they have been working increasingly closely. Since 1988 they have had common "priority objectives". These are:

"1 promoting the development and structural adjustment of the regions whose development is lagging behind (hereinafter referred to as 'Objective 1');

2 converting the regions, frontier regions or parts of regions (including employment areas and urban communities) seriously affected by industrial decline (hereinafter referred to as 'Objective 2');

3 combatting long-term unemployment (hereinafter referred to as 'Objective 3');

4 facilitating the occupational integration of young people (hereinafter referred to as 'Objective 4');

5 with a view to reform of the common agricultural policy:
(a) speeding up the adjustment of agricultural structures, and
(b) promoting the development of rural areas
(hereinafter referred to as 'Objective 5(a) and 5(b)')."

(Council Regulation (EEC) No 2052/88 of 24th June 1988)

As far as the United Kingdom is concerned, only Northern Ireland is designated as Objective 1. The Objective 2 and Objective 5(b) areas are listed in box page 40.

The 1992 budget for the Structural Funds is almost £15 billion. In Objective 1 areas, the European Community will contribute up to three-quarters of the cost of the work carried out. Elsewhere the contribution from the Community is unlikely to exceed 50% (45% in the case of the European Social Fund). Money from the Structural Funds is supposed to be "additional". That means they should not be used to reduce a national government's own contribution. This has been an area of dispute between the Commission and the UK government over the years and in early 1992 the Commission delayed payment of some grants until it had assurances from the Government that the funds would be accounted for in a way that made their additionality clear.

The European Structural Funds are run on the basis of programmes agreed between national governments and the Commission of the European Communities. These programmes specify the sort of activities that will be funded in each region. Most of the money supports the programmes of national or local government but other organisations are eligible and, in the United Kingdom in particular, many do so. Organisations that wish to apply for finance from the Structural Funds should contact an agency appointed by the UK government. Normally for sports organisations this will be a local authority consortium but it is possible that some applications for the European Social Fund could go to the National Council for Voluntary Organisations. Other sources of advice or information include the local offices of the Department of the Environment, the Department of Trade and Industry, the Scottish Office and the Welsh Office.

The European Structural Funds are under review at present and new arrangements are expected to be in force from January 1994. At the time of writing, the indications are that substantial changes will not be made at this review. It is felt that the arrangements agreed in 1988 have only just become fully established and that they should not be altered much before a further review in about five years' time.

The European Structural Funds – Priority Areas in the UK
(see box on previous page for an explanation of the "Objectives")

UK area coming under Objective 1 category: Northern Ireland

Objective 2 areas in the UK: All of Cleveland, Durham, Greater Manchester, Merseyside, Mid-Glamorgan, South Yorkshire, Tyne and Wear, West Glamorgan and West Midlands **and parts of:** Central, Cheshire, Clwyd, Cumbria, Derbyshire, Dumfries and Galloway, Dyfed, Fife, Gwent, Humberside, Lancashire, Lincolnshire, Lothian, Northumberland, North Yorkshire, Nottinghamshire, Powys, Shropshire, South Glamorgan, Staffordshire, Strathclyde, Tayside, West Yorkshire and Warwickshire.
The European Structural Funds actually use 'Travel to Work' areas. Your local authority should be able to tell you whether or not you are in a Travel to Work area which is covered.

Objective 5(b) areas in the UK: All of Dumfries and Galloway and the Highlands and Islands Development Board area **and parts of** Cornwall, Devon, Dyfed, Galloway, Gwynedd and Powys. Once again you need to know your Travel to Work area in these counties.

information. In simple cases, the call specifies a date by which bids for the work have to be returned. A committee then decides which tender to accept, paying attention to both cost and experience of the organisations submitting tenders.

Grant procedures

Most sports organisations will not need to go through those complications. The majority of grants schemes are dealt with by a relatively simple application form, available from the contacts listed for each scheme. The contact will also give you up-to-date information about when the best time to submit applications will be. In very general terms, this is often in November, when you can either get high on the list for action in the following year or, with luck, pick up some funds made available at short notice by, for example, some other applicant not taking up a grant.

Following up applications

The administration of most grant schemes is the responsibility of the Commission. Explicit lobbying of the Commission or its agents can be counter productive. However, it is important that you keep as many people as possible informed about your application and its progress. You should certainly include in this some MEPs, the local office of the Commission (see box page 74), national civil servants, your local authority and, possibly the UK Representation in Brussels (see Appendix 7). In addition, if you have the good luck to be in contact with any senior people at the Commission, you should be sure that they know about your application. Grant schemes are designed not to need applicants to visit Brussels. However in a few cases, where large grants are at stake, the process can certainly be facilitated with a visit to the relevant official. You should take the opportunity to visit other key people, including MEPs and UKREP (see Chapter 3 on lobbying).

Chapter  6

Grants for international events and exchanges

Exchange programmes

Many European Community programmes are intended to promote our sense of being European or to assist **exchanges of people and experience** between one part of the Community and another. At present none of these programmes are specifically intended to assist sports people but neither are sports-related exchanges excluded. Within the Commission, the grants described in this chapter are administered either by Directorate-General X (Audiovisual, Information, Communication and Culture) or by the Secretariat-General.

Many of the training and education programmes mentioned in the next chapter also have money for exchanges. Similarly the programmes directed at people with special needs may also be able to help.

6-1

Support for Sports Events from the Public Awareness Budget

DG X funding

Directorate-General X (Audiovisual, Information, Communication and Culture) of the EC Commission has a budget (which totalled approximately £5 million in 1992) for "an all-round drive in the area of communication, campaigns and events for the general public associated with Community events, and participation in sports events". The whole exercise is meant "to strengthen European citizens' feeling of belonging to the Community" (quotes from the EC budget). In 1992 almost £1 million was allocated to sports activities.

Funding for sports events

This budget is used in part to contribute to the costs of **sports events**. Until recently the Commission favoured promoting new events (see the upper box opposite). Today, however, it prefers to make a modest contribution to ensure that an existing event has a European dimension. The 1992 Tour de France, for example, received a grant from the Commission. The Community is associated with it in the public eye and the Tour visited a total of seven Community countries. The lower box opposite below gives a few examples of the use of this money. The box on page 44 shows the way the Commission justifies these grants to, not always friendly, MEPs. The Commission is used to working in collaboration with commercial sponsors. It will not, however, contribute to an event which is associated with the names of distillers or with tobacco products.

Criteria for grants

Size of grants

Notwithstanding the emphasis on larger events, smaller ones are still eligible. The **two fixed criteria** are that the event supported must have a substantial European dimension and that there is likely to be considerable media interest in it. **The grants given normally fall into the range £1 000 to £200 000.** Applications start their way through the decision-making structures as soon as they are received. In the future it is hoped to change to a system where there would be a fixed date for applications which would then go before a specially appointed panel for decision.

European Community Swimming Club Championships

In 1993 Greece will be using what is claimed to be the finest Olympic pool in the world to host the seventh annual European Community Swimming Club Championships with financial support from the Commission of the European Community. Derek Stubbs, Director of Swimming for the Amateur Swimming Association, is the Secretary of the small steering group which negotiates with the Commission on behalf of the swimming associations of the twelve countries of the EC. In November 1985 the Commission invited representatives of the swimming associations of the then 10 countries (Portugal and Spain joined the following year) to Brussels to discuss the possibility of establishing a European Community Swimming Championship. The initial idea of an individual championship was soon discarded as being too close in concept to the European Championship open to the thirty or so countries of the wider Europe.

Agreement was reached, however, on a club championship. Each country's swimming federation holds separate club championships for men and for women. The winning teams from each country then compete in the European Community club championship. The first of the series was held in Leeds in 1987. This was a major sporting and publicity success and attracted many European dignitaries including the relevant member of the Commission of the European Community. The Commission's financial contribution, which amounted to some £100 000, helped with the administration costs and enabled the organisers to cover the travel and accommodation costs of all the participants – some 300 people.

This support has continued at almost the same level annually since 1987. Each year a different country (Luxembourg in 1988, then Hamburg, Milan, Amsterdam and, in 1992, Toulouse) takes on the responsibility for organising the championship. General coordination and negotiations with the Commission are in the hands of a small group composed of a chairperson, a secretary and representatives of the hosting federations for the current year and the following year. In addition all twelve countries come together for a business meeting at the time of the full European calendar conference.

Examples of the Use of the EC Public Awareness Budget for Sports Events:

European Community Swimming Club Championships (see box above)

Tour de France

European School Games

European Youth Olympics

European Yacht Race

Euro Cycling Tour

Rugby Union World Cup (see box page 44)

European Network of Sports Sciences in Higher Education (see box page 52)

Rugby Union Sponsorship

On 8th November 1991 Terence Wynn (MEP for Merseyside East) asked the Commission:

"How much money has the Commission given to the Rugby Union World Cup organizers to have the European flag symbol displayed on ground perimeter advertising hoardings?

From what budget line was this taken?"

On 3rd March 1992 Commissioner Dondelinger gave the reply:-

"The Commission's contribution was made in response to a request from the Rugby Union World Cup organizers. It consisted of ECU 10 000 and the 18 European flags used to decorate the grounds.

More than a million spectators watched the matches, which were broadcast to 58 countries for over two billion television viewers.

The cost was charged to budget item B3-3030."

Advice for applicants

If you are promoting the European or World Championships in your sport and if you expect good media coverage it may be worth your while applying for support. Other activities with a strong "European dimension" may also be funded. For all applications you should contact:

Mr Gian Pietro Fontana-Rava, DG X/C/4, Commission of the European Communities, 200 Rue de la Loi, 1049 Brussels, Belgium
Tel: 010 32 2 299 9366, Fax: 010 32 2 299 9284

You should send information about the event, its purpose and scale and about its European aspects. This should be accompanied by a budget expressed in ecu (see page 38) which shows clearly what support is requested from the European Community.

It is also worth approaching the office of the Commission in the country of the event. Some of these funds are allocated to the offices for use at their discretion.

Special budgets for large events

On some occasions the European Parliament votes a special budget allocation to allow a more substantial contribution to be made. This is not something that many sports organisations will be involved with. Arranging for it to happen is a matter of lobbying and much of the advice in Chapter 5 will not apply. Refer instead to Chapter 3. Recent EC grants to the 1992 Barcelona Olympics and 1991 World Student Games in Sheffield came under this category.

6-2

Town Twinning

Town twinning links often include a sporting element. Normally the local communities concerned are expected to cover the costs involved but financial assistance can be available under some conditions. In particular, the European Community has **funds to support twinning** between communities. Priority goes to those which are at a disadvantage because they are remote, because their language is not widely spoken or because they are in a country which has only recently acceded to the European Community. In 1992 the funds available were about £3 million. These were mainly intended to support twinning between towns within the Community but a small proportion was reserved for links between the European Community and towns in central and eastern Europe.

For full information contact your local authority or the:
Twinning Officer, Local Government International Bureau, 35 Great Smith Street, London SW1P 3BJ
Tel: 071 222 1636, Fax: 071 233 2179

Funds for sport within twinning programmes

6-3

Support for International Non-Governmental Youth Organisations

The Commission provides support for international non-governmental youth organisations that promote the European dimension. This could include a genuinely European youth sports organisation. **Typically grants are about £6 000**.

Applications are made to the Secretariat-General of the Commission on a form which is available from them. The closing date is 30th April of the year for which a grant is requested.

Contact:
Mr Brian Owen, Secretariat-General, Commission of the European Communities, 200 Rue de la Loi, 1049 Brussels, Belgium
Tel: 010 32 2 235 4742, Fax: 010 32 2 236 2389

Grants for pan-European youth groups

Chapter 7

Grants for training, education and research

Programmes for improving employment prospects

Improving employment prospects and particularly training for jobs has been a major European Community pre-occupation for many years. This shows itself in a stream of reports and policy statements. It is also expressed in a number of the grant programmes. More recently, Community work in the broad field of education has blossomed and the need to support research has become widely accepted.

The schemes described in this chapter are likely to be of interest to only a minority of sports organisations. Those organisations which are engaged in the relevant areas will find that funding can be on a substantial scale. Within the Commission, the officials who run the European Social Fund are in Directorate-General V (Employment, Industrial Relations and Social Affairs). Research is the responsibility of Directorate-General XII (Science, Research and Development) who publish an excellent guide called 'EC Research Funding' (see box page 77). The other schemes are within the area of the Task Force for Human Resources, Education, Training and Youth.

7·1
European Social Fund

Programmes to create vocational training schemes

The European Social Fund is one of the **Structural Funds** (see box page 39). It provides part funding for certain schemes of **vocational training** and, to a much smaller extent, for wage subsidy schemes. The vocational training should be intended to equip unemployed people with the skills they need to undertake identified jobs – though the actual vacancies do not normally need to be known in advance. The grants are allocated through government departments and, except in Northern Ireland, through intermediary operators of various kinds. In Great Britain, most sports organisations would apply either through local authority channels (see box opposite for a case study) or through the National Council for Voluntary Organisations. The allocation of grants follows priorities that are determined partly at the level of the European Community, partly at the national level and partly at the level of the intermediary operator.

Priority regions and target groups

These **priorities** are based upon geographical considerations and upon the particular difficulties of the groups of people being trained. Thus Northern Ireland has the highest priority. The areas of industrial decline in Scotland and the North of England also have a high priority. So do women returning to work, people with disabilities and people who have been out of work for a very long period. Other factors can also give priority. Some examples are:
• elements of innovation;
• links with other European Community countries; and
• whether the training leads to nationally recognised qualifications.

Specialist programmes

In some cases the European Community has identified an area of sufficient concern for it to launch a special European Social Fund initiative. Three current examples are **HORIZON** (for people with disabilities, people facing particular poverty and refugees), **NOW** (aimed to help women take full advantage on equal terms of economic growth and technological development) and **EUROFORM** (for training in new occupations, new opportunities and new skills).

Comsport Project – Training Women for Sports Leadership

Comsport is a Sports Development project supported by the Sports Council and run by Northamptonshire County Council. During 1992 it ran two courses for women to qualify as sports leaders. The total cost was estimated to be almost £30 000 of which the European Social Fund was expected to contribute 45%.

'Confident Women Lead' came into being because Comsport had discovered a shortage of qualified sports leaders (particularly exercise to music tutors) for its village recreation projects. Thus work is assured for many of the successful trainees. Women were identified particularly for this project because the work fits well with family commitments and because the selected areas of Northamptonshire have high rates of unemployment among women.

Vocational training to enable women to take male dominated jobs is one of the priorities for the European Social Fund. Comsport therefore decided to submit an application for ESF funding through the County Council and FEMLA – the Federation of East Midlands Local Authorities. Anne Rippon of the Sports Council's East Midlands office and Judith Percival of Comsport were responsible for translating the project description into a completed ESF application form. They were greatly helped by Northamptonshire's European Officer who submitted the application to FEMLA. Information was supplied about unemployment in the county (which strengthened the application) and gave advice about how to fill in the form. Anne Rippon's advice to anyone considering the use of the ESF is to make early contact with their local authority's European officer.

The application was submitted in September 1991, when it was hoped that a decision would be made early in 1992. The first of the two courses started in Daventry in January 1992 with 29 trainees. It was not until the end of May, however, that Comsport heard that its application had been approved. The first payment was not received until August. In the meantime the project was running on money made available by the Sports Council and Northamptonshire County Council. In effect the ESF enabled Comsport to run two courses instead of just one.

The trainees were recruited by word of mouth and by press advertisements. Take up of both the Daventry course and the second one in Northampton exceeded expectations. The trainees worked towards the CCPR Sports Leader Award, an Emergency First Aid Certificate and, normally, an RSA Basic Certificate in Exercise to Music. In some cases the training was for leadership in other sports. In all cases, the training was supplemented with assertiveness training and business skills.

Further applications for European Community money for women and perhaps for people from ethnic minorities are planned for the future.

Requirements to match grants

Amount of grant

The European Social Fund has large sums available to it but they have to be matched by other public sector funding in Great Britain to the extent of 55%. For this purpose money from any central or local government agency and certain charitable foundations can count. One of the sources of public money has also to be willing to guarantee that the project will be completed. For most sports organisations, it will be the availability of matching funds that limits the amount they can apply for. Typically **grants for non-governmental organisations would be in the range £10 000 to £100 000 per annum**.

Timetable for applications

The main European Social Fund allocates grants one year at a time. The year runs from 1st January to 31st December and applications for one year normally need to be submitted the previous September in a process which involves the completion of several forms with close attention to detail. The initiatives mentioned above are exceptions in that applications are sought from time to time and that successful projects can expect to be funded over a period of two or three years.

For further information about the European Social Fund contact the European Community specialist in your local authority or:
National Council for Voluntary Organisations, Regent's Wharf,
8 All Saints Street, London N1 9RL
Tel: 071 713 6161, Fax: 071 713 6300

In Northern Ireland all applicants should contact:
European Community Branch, Department of Economic Development,
The Arches Centre, 11-13 Bloomfield Avenue, Belfast BT5 5HD
Tel: 0232 732411 x316

7-2

FORCE

Partnership schemes for vocational training

The aim of the FORCE programme is the promotion of company-based **continuing vocational training**. It works through partnerships of companies, training bodies, trade unions and employers' organisations.

Funds available

In 1992 FORCE had a budget of **about £13.5 million**. Most of this was spent on the support of transnational training projects, including exchanges, pilot projects and skills analysis projects. Competition for support is sharp – in 1992 782 applications were made but only 263 were selected for support. **Support for a training project varies but would typically be of the order of £35 000**.

Any sports organisation which employs significant numbers of staff could use support from the FORCE programme to work with colleagues from other European Community countries on improving the skills of their staff (see box opposite for an example).

Contact:

Technical Assistance Office, FORCE, Rue du Nord 34, 1000 Brussels, Belgium
Tel: 010 32 2 209 1311, Fax: 010 32 2 209 1320
or
Mr Will Thompson, FORCE UK National Co-ordination Unit, Employment
Department, Room E315, Moorfoot, Sheffield S1 4PQ
Tel: 0742 594819, Fax: 0742 594103

Health, Fitness and Sports Therapy – Collaboration between the Spa Regions of Europe

Sara Lloyd of Coleg Powys in Llandrindod Wells is at the centre of a FORCE project which brings Llandrindod Wells together with spa regions in France, Italy and Germany. The aim of the project is to build on a previous European Social Fund scheme which trained leisure centre staff. The FORCE project will establish a European consortium to carry out a training needs analysis. This will identify the skills needed to qualify leisure centre staff to set up fitness therapies. Where possible the existing national qualifications will be compared.

The process of applying for FORCE support created considerable pressure. In 1992 only about 10% of applications were successful. The Technical Assistance Office in Brussels was helpful on the mechanics of applying but it was found that there was considerable work involved in designing the project and in finding suitable partners. It was only made manageable by the fact that the previous project had already put Ms Lloyd in touch with the key partner organisations.

7-3

PETRA Action I

PETRA is the European Community's programme which aims to prepare **young people** between 16 and 27 for working life. Action I, described here, covers **exchanges between Member States** of the Community. Action II (see page 60) provides support for training projects that wish to take part in a European Community network. It also includes the support of projects started by young people. Action III is concerned with the development of networks of people working on the vocational guidance of young people.

Exchanges for young people

"Action I" of PETRA has two main activities, either of which could be of interest to sports organisations which train or employ young people. The first is for young people undergoing **vocational training** between school and starting work which leads to a nationally recognised qualification. It enables them to undertake a placement in another European Community country. This placement is normally for a **three week period**.

Vocational training placements

The second main activity provides young people with the opportunity to live and work abroad. This is intended to widen their vocational skills and improve their language skills. The young people concerned stay abroad, normally, for **3 months** and either undertake work placement or vocational training. It is not available to university students or graduates.

Amount of grant available

In both cases financial assistance will not exceed organisational costs, some language training, subsistence while in another country and three-quarters of the travel costs. **For short-term placements this is typically about £500. For long-term placements a figure of about £2 000 would be normal.**

The European Network for Sports Sciences in Higher Education

In order to further promote ERASMUS activities in sports studies, a co-ordinating group has been established. The European Network for Sports Sciences in Higher Education includes members from each of the twelve states of the European Communities. Commissions have been established to gather and co-ordinate information in the following areas:

1 The formulation of a European University Institute of Sports Sciences: A European Master's Degree (1 year) and a European Certificate (Summer School) are anticipated.

2 European courses of study in sports sciences.

3 Vocational/professional studies and qualifications in sports sciences. The relationships between university structures and other related organisations (sports schools, coaching institutes). This group is also promoting information exchanges with related organisations, such as The Council of Europe and the Delbeccha Group of sports ministers.

The Network aims to promote exchanges; it hopes to achieve this aim by publicising the opportunities available, and by bringing together institutions with shared interest to form organising consortia.

A directory has been published, outlining each national structure and listing each institution with a potential interest in exchange arrangements.

A Forum for the representatives of institutions interested in exchange arrangements was held in Lisbon (October 1991) and a further Forum will be held in Cologne from 8-12 September 1993.

Finally, a Network Bulletin is distributed to all interested institutions, describing progress to date and calling for expressions of interest in areas of collaborative teaching and research.

It will be seen that the Network is centred around the ERASMUS programme. It has already received ERASMUS funding for some of its working meetings. It has also received grants from the budget for public awareness that is administered by Directorate-General X (Audiovisual, Information, Communication and Culture).

At the time of writing, both the status of informal European networks and the mechanisms by which their deliberations might be incorporated into the overall Community decision-making process are unclear.

Applications should be sent to:
Ms Jane Owen, PETRA National Co-ordination Unit, Central Bureau for Educational Visits and Exchanges, Seymour Mews House, Seymour Mews, London W1H 9PE
Tel: 071 486 5101, Fax: 071 935 5741

Ms Owen can supply further information on deadlines and eligibility. The National Co-ordination Unit can help with finding partners in other Member States, but cannot guarantee a timescale on this.

7-4

Youth for Europe

Youth for Europe is a European community programme in the field of education. Its main activity is the **encouragement and support of exchanges** of people between the ages of 15 and 25. These exchanges should involve a structured programme of instruction about some aspect of the experience of being in another country and another culture and of working in another language. Sports activities could certainly be part of an exchange under the Youth for Europe programme but they are unlikely to be the principal focus of one.

Cultural exchange programmes for young people

Grants are available for projects which involve young people from at least two European Community* countries coming together to live and study. This should involve a total of between 16 and 20 young people working together on a project lasting at least 6 full days. The actual participants should be involved in all stages from preparation and planning to evaluation and follow up. At least a third of the available funds go to projects involving young people who would otherwise find it difficult to take part in an exchange for financial, social or geographical reasons. **The maximum grant is about £18 000.**

Need for European dimension

Amount of grant available

The administration of the programme is undertaken at national level. Organisations wishing to take part should contact:
Ms Hilary Jarman, Youth Exchange Centre, The British Council,
10 Spring Gardens, London SW1A 2BN
Tel: 071 389 4030, Fax: 071 389 4033

* This will be extended to all European Economic Area (EEA) countries as soon as the EEA treaty enters into force (expected 1st January 1993). See Appendix 3 for a list of the EEA countries.

7-5

Exchange of School Teachers

The European Community has a scheme to encourage inter-disciplinary **projects between schools in different Community countries**. Under this scheme it

Travel grants for teachers

is able to provide **grants, typically of about £1 000, to teachers** spending three or four weeks on exchange in the other school. There is no bar to sports teachers taking part, if they are involved in the project. Grants can cover travel, subsistence and the cost of joint projects.

For further details and application forms contact:

Ms Vicky Gough, Central Bureau, Seymour Mews House,
Seymour Mews, London W1H 9PE
Tel: 071 486 5101, Fax: 071 935 5741

7-6
ERASMUS

Funds for co-operation projects

ERASMUS budget

ERASMUS is a programme for **higher education** institutions. It provides financial support for co-operation between universities and similar organisations: it provides **grants for staff visits and student mobility** and limited funding is available for supporting European associations of higher education institutions, for publications designed to increase awareness of the possibilities for mobility in higher education and for exchanges of information related to academic recognition and course credit transfers. **About £56 million was available for ERASMUS in 1992.**

Institutions concerned with sports science or sports medicine may be interested in a number of programmes.

Application criteria and procedures

Grants are given for **staff visits**, which can cover study, preparatory visits and meetings and teaching visits. The visits must be to institutions in another country in the European Community or in the European Free Trade Area. Applications need to be made at least six months before the date of travel. Applications are processed quarterly in groups so applications made by 1st April 1993 will have a decision by June.

Co-operation programmes are agreed for a period of up to three years. They should focus on one subject area. "Physical Education, Sports Science" is an obvious one but some sports-related work could also be included under, for example, teacher training or medical science. The programmes can cover student exchanges, staff exchanges, the development of new curricula and "intensive programmes" – which are short teaching programmes bringing together students and teaching staff from several countries. The institutions involved in the programmes must come from different countries of the European Community or the European Free Trade Area. Applications for the 93/94 academic year were due in by 31st October 1992. It is expected that the deadline for the 94/95 year will be October 93.

Support for European associations

Funds are available for projects of specific academic interest within a European context. The box page 52 gives one example of how this works. Applications

are processed quarterly in groups so applications made by 1st April 1993 will have a decision by June.

The ERASMUS programme is organised by:
The ERASMUS Bureau, 70 Rue Montoyer, 1040 Brussels, Belgium
Tel: 010 32 2 233 0111, Fax: 010 32 2 233 0150

7-7

TEMPUS

TEMPUS is the European Community's scheme of assistance for the development of **higher education** in some of the countries of **Eastern and Central Europe** (see box below for the list) and for promoting the interaction between universities in those countries and European Community partners. It is structured around programmes and visits in much the same way as ERASMUS (see previous section). However, in 1993/4 the only subject areas of obvious interest to sports organisations are health and, in a few countries, teacher education.

For full details contact either:
EC TEMPUS Office, 14 Rue Montoyer, 1040 Brussels, Belgium
Tel: 010 32 2 504 0711, Fax: 010 32 2 504 0700
or
Europe Unit, Education and Science Division, The British Council,
Medlock Street, Manchester M15 4AA
Tel: 061 957 7074/6, Fax: 061 957 7561

Exchanges with Eastern Europe

Eastern and Central European Countries Eligible for Support under the TEMPUS Scheme	
Albania	Latvia
Bulgaria	Lithuania
Czech & Slovak Federal Republic	Poland
Estonia	Romania
Hungary	Slovenia

7-8

Biomedical and Health Research

The European Community is running a multi-annual research programme in this area which might be of interest to an academic specialist in **sports medicine**. For example, an application could be made for a programme involving institutions in several EC countries and, perhaps involving some non-EC European countries, which looked at new ways of using sport in the

Grants for research work

treatment of people injured at work or as a means of slowing the ageing process. **Funds might be available for meetings, exchanges, joint data handling and dissemination** and, to a limited extent, for the actual research costs.

Limited availability of grants

The competition for these grants is particularly intense. In 1992 only one hundred applications were successful out of 1 900 submitted. Programmes need to be clearly focussed and the trans-national element is essential with the European dimension clearly explained. Applications are made in response to occasional announcements in the Official Journal. For full information contact:

Mrs G Breen, Medical Research Council, 20 Park Crescent, London W1N 4AL
Tel: 071 636 5422, Fax: 071 436 6179
or
Dr Anthony Dickens, DG XII/F/6, Commission of the European Communities,
200 Rue de la Loi, 1049 Brussels, Belgium
Tel: 010 32 2 235 0032, Fax: 010 32 2 235 5365

Chapter (8)

Grants for facilities and new enterprises

Grants from the Commission

This chapter brings together information about a number of grant schemes which could be used for the development of **sports facilities** and some which can help with the **start-up costs of new enterprises**. They are drawn from various parts of the Commission. It is important to note that the Regional Development Fund has its own Directorate-General – number XVI. The grants for conservation are administered by Directorate-General X, farm diversification by DG VI, LIFE by DG XI, tourism falls to DG XXIII and the other two are in the remit of the Task Force for Human Resources, Education, Training and Youth.

There have been many examples of the **European Regional Development Fund assisting with the costs of sports facilities**. The other schemes listed in this chapter are potential sources of money, but, as far as is known, sports organisations have yet to take advantage of them.

8-1

European Regional Development Fund

Areas eligible for ERDF

The European Regional Development Fund (ERDF) is one of the **Structural Funds** (see box page 39). It provides assistance with projects in **areas suffering from underdevelopment** (Northern Ireland in the UK) **or from industrial decline** (see box page 40 for a list of the UK areas covered). In addition some inner city areas have been able to secure some European Regional Development Fund support. From time to time the European Commission has identified other areas that need assistance with economic development and areas facing a decline, in particular industrial sectors. Thus the **RECHAR initiative helps areas where the coal industry is running down** and **RENAVAL is for former ship-building areas. INTERREG provides assistance in border areas.**

Some Examples of the Use of the ERDF for Sports Facilities

Scottish National Water Skiing Centre

Tennis Centres at Nottingham and Bodmin

Leisure Centres at Welshpool, Barmouth, Torquay, Falkirk and Renfrew

The Fife Coast Footpath and the Five Weirs Walk and Cycleway in Sheffield

The INTERREG programme for the border area between Northern Ireland and the Republic contains a specific mention of support for "sports tourism"

International Athletic Stadium and Indoor Arena at Sheffield for the 1991 World Student Games (see box opposite) and in July 1992 the Commission adopted a programme which includes facilities for Manchester's Olympic bid

RECHAR funding has been provided for the provision of a swimming pool at Hucknall, Nottinghamshire and also for the construction of squash courts and refurbishment of a swimming pool at Cresswell, Derbyshire

---

The European Regional Development Fund assistance is intended to contribute to the economic development of the area concerned. This means that sports projects which get support tend to do so on the grounds of their **contribution to the local tourist industry**. Thus leisure pools and tennis centres have had support in the past. Some examples are mentioned in the box opposite. See also the case study of the Sheffield World Student Games in the box below.

Criteria for support

In the United Kingdom the European Regional Development Fund is administered by:
The Department of Trade and Industry, Regional Development and Inward Investment Division, Room 317, Kingsgate House, 66-74 Victoria Street, London SW1E 6SW
Tel: 071 215 2611, Fax: 071 215 8779

In virtually all cases, however, the key to access to the European Regional Development Fund will lie with the relevant local authority and sports organisations are advised to contact them for help.

World Student Games – Sheffield 1991

In July 1991 Sheffield was host to the Universiade – the World Student Games. For these games and for community use, the city built the Ponds Forge International Sports Centre with a technically advanced 50 metre swimming pool, the Don Valley International Athletics Stadium and the Don Valley Indoor Arena.

On the grounds that these facilities contributed to the economic and environmental revival of the Lower Don Valley, the city was able to secure a European Regional Development Fund contribution towards £65 million of the costs.

As a separate exercise, Sheffield was able to persuade Members of the European Parliament to vote 1 million ecu (about £700 000 at the time) for general support of the organisation and for ensuring that the European Community was publicly associated with the Games.

8-2
Conservation of the European Architectural Heritage

The Commission runs an annual award scheme to encourage good practice in the conservation of the architectural heritage. This is restricted to sites which are open to the public. Each year the scheme has a **particular theme** – historical gardens and green spaces in 1993. The exact rules change from year to year though normally applications need to be submitted before, or very early in the year to which they apply.

Criteria for support

The size of the award varies from project to project but under any circumstances, the **award is not more than 25% of the total cost** of the

Maximum grant available

restoration work in the year in question – which can be extended to the September following the calendar year end. It is possible to apply for projects which are already under way, but grants will not be made in respect of the work carried out in previous years. **In any case no grant is for more than about £100 000**.

This scheme might be of interest to an organisation which was developing a facility on a heritage site. For full details contact:
Commission of the European Communities, DG X, Culture Unit,
200 Rue de la Loi (T/120), 1049 Brussels, Belgium
Tel: 010 32 2 299 9247, Fax: 010 32 2 299 9283
Applications need to be submitted both to the Culture Unit and to one of the following:
English Heritage, Fortress House, 23 Savile Row, London WC1X 1AB
Historic Scotland, 20 Brandon Street, Edinburgh EH3 5RA
CADW, Brunel House, 2 Fitzalan Road, Cardiff CF2 1UY
Historic Monuments and Buildings Branch, 5-33 Hill Street, Belfast BT1 1LA

8-3
LIFE

New programme for countryside and environment projects

LIFE is a new European Community programme of financial assistance to projects contributing to the development of the Community's **environment** policies. At the time of writing the details of the management of this scheme have not been decided but it is expected that applications for one year will need to be submitted by October of the previous year. LIFE includes programmes on the protection of habitats and the protection of northern coastal waters, but the part most likely to interest sports organisations concerns the integration of environmental factors into land use planning. Sports organisations, perhaps those who use the countryside as a facility, may feel that some aspect of their work would fit this category.

Competition for grants from LIFE is expected to be intense, so interested organisations would be well advised to make informal soundings before spending much time on an application.

For information and application procedures contact:
Mr Richard Longman, Environmental Protection Central Division, Department of the Environment, Room B242, 43 Marsham Street, London SW1P 3PY
Tel: 071 276 8146, Fax: 071 276 8626

8-4
PETRA Action II

Training projects for young people

PETRA is the European Community's programme which aims to prepare young people, aged 16 to 27, for working life. Action I (see page 51) covers exchanges. Action II provides **support for training projects that wish to take part in a European Community network**. It also includes the support of projects organised and run by young people. Action III is concerned with the development of networks of people working on the vocational guidance of young people.

Vocational guidance for young people

The main activity under PETRA Action II is the European Network of Training Partnerships which supports the joint development (between EC countries) of training modules and the joint training of trainers. Of greater interest in the sports context may be the provision for the support of Youth Initiative Projects.

A **Youth Initiative Project** is one both developed and carried out by young people. It should be innovative and intended to promote creativity, initiative and enterprise and it should help the young people involved to get access to vocational training or paid employment. Projects should normally operate for at least one year and priority is given to those which:

Youth Initiative Projects

- help young people in difficulty;
- improve young people's competencies in the use of the media and the new technologies;
- help young people to create new jobs;
- promote equal opportunities for girls and young women;
- make official bodies aware of the needs of young people.

Priority themes

The maximum grant is about £7 000 or 50% of the total costs. It is non-renewable.

Amount of grant available

For further information and application forms contact:
Mr Jason Forsythe, PETRA National Co-ordination Unit, Central Bureau for Educational Visits and Exchanges, Seymour Mews House, Seymour Mews, London W1H 9PE
Tel: 071 486 5101, Fax: 071 935 5741

8-5
Youth Pilot Projects

The Commission runs a number of "Priority Actions in the Youth Field". One of these may be of interest to sports organisations working with young people. Grants for Youth Pilot Projects are available to projects which last between one month and twelve months. The range of activities that could be covered is wide and specifically includes **leisure and cultural activities**.
Youth Pilot Projects must:

Youth schemes not involving employment

- be innovative;
- involve interesting methods;
- be local (or regional) initiatives;

- be managed by the young people themselves;
- respond to the needs and interests of young people and, therefore,
- be likely to interest young people in other European Community countries.

If a grant is made it will not exceed half the total cost of the project unless the young people concerned are disadvantaged (perhaps by facing poverty or by living in an economically depressed or remote area or because they have disabilities or belong to a minority group...). In this case the grant can be as much as three-quarters of the total cost.

Priority themes

Priority is given to Youth Pilot Projects which reflect the ethnic, cultural and linguistic reality of the local community. The projects should encourage young people to become more aware of their belonging to the European Community, but there is **no requirement for another country to be involved**.

This scheme seems to be complementary to the Youth Initiative Projects which can be funded under PETRA II (see previous section). Whereas PETRA is specifically linked to helping young people to join the workforce, Youth Pilot Projects are excluded from being explicitly linked to work, neither can they be school-related.

For further details contact:
European Community Youth Exchange Bureau, 2-3 Place du Luxembourg, 1040 Brussels, Belgium
Tel: 010 32 2 511 1510, Fax: 010 32 2 511 1960

Submission dates for 1993 have not been announced at the time of writing. In any case applications will need to be submitted at least two months in advance.

8-6
Farm Diversification

Grants for changes to use of farm lands

Funds are available from the European Structural Funds (see box page 39) for assistance to farmers who wish to take on other forms of business. **"Rural tourism"** is particularly mentioned in this context. This could certainly be seen to cover the use of former agricultural land for some sporting purposes but not those involving mechanically propelled vehicles or firearms.

For information and application forms contact:
Ministry of Agriculture, Fisheries and Food, Rural Structures and Grants Division, Nobel House, 17 Smith Square, London SW1P 3RJ
Tel: 071 238 5367, Fax: 071 238 6591

Chapter ⑨

Grants for people with special needs

Each of the grant schemes described in this chapter is tightly focussed on a group of people that the European Community has recognised as having special needs which must be met if they are to play their full role in the economy and in society. Only in one case is sport particularly mentioned but the officials administering the other schemes are open to the idea that sport has a contribution to make.

Most of these schemes are **modest** in scale. In many cases more help is available for the groups concerned through, for example, the European Structural Funds. Directorate-General V (Employment, Industrial Relations and Social Affairs) is the key section of the Commission for all these grants except TIDE, which is part of the work of Directorate-General XIII (Tele-communications, Information Industries and Innovation).

9-1

HELIOS

Programme for people with disabilities

HELIOS is the European Community's main activity specifically intended for **people with disabilities**. It is concerned with their work and living conditions and is divided into programmes. The programmes cover:
- networks of local activities in favour of people with disabilities;
- a network of rehabilitation centres;
- an information network (Handynet);
- an award scheme to recognise good practice in the provision of mobility and transport, access to public buildings and housing.

The HELIOS programme was under revision at the time of writing and is expected to cover health promotion programmes. Few sports organisations are likely to take part in the HELIOS networks but the award scheme category on

---

Go-Karts for People with Disabilities

The Danish Sports Organisation for the Disabled (DSOD) won a HELIOS award in 1990 in the category "Transport and Mobility". This was in recognition of their development of a go-kart which opens the possibility of enjoying the sport to many disabled people.

Their go-kart is based on a standard machine but the accelerator and brake pedals and the steering wheel have been replaced by two joy sticks – rather similar to the controls used for radio-controlled model cars. The go-kart also has a clutch, enabling the user to stop with the engine still running. It is capable of speeds in excess of 40mph and is now in commercial production.

Kristian Jensen of the DSOD commented that the preparation for the award had involved a lot of work producing the necessary papers, photographs and a video. The main advantage to DSOD was in the boost to the interest of the Danish media in the project.

access to public buildings may be of interest to organisations with facilities which have made efforts to integrate people with disabilities (see box opposite).

HELIOS has a technical assistance office in Brussels:
HELIOS, 79 Avenue de Cortenberg, 1040 Brussels, Belgium
Tel: 010 32 2 735 4105, Fax: 010 32 2 735 1671

There is also a network of national contacts. For the United Kingdom contact:
Mr Warren Brown, Department of Health, Waterloo Road, London SE1 8UG
Tel: 071 972 4126, Fax: 071 972 4132

9-2
EUCREA – support for cultural projects involving people with disabilities

EUCREA is a non-governmental organisation which uses HELIOS funding to organise an annual round of support for **cultural projects**. These involve people with disabilities from at least four European Community countries. Projects have to be innovative and add to the variety and richness of European cultural life. There is scope for some sporting activities to fall into the area of culture. **Grants are typically about £5 000**.

Cultural programmes for people with disabilities

Size of grants

United Kingdom applications need to be submitted through the National Disability Arts Forum by the end of September of the previous year. Each year has a special theme, which for 1993 is "Information-Communication-Media".

Contact:
Katherine Walsh, National Disability Arts Forum, 28 Coombes Lane, Northfield, Birmingham B31 4QW

9-3
Sporting Events for People with Disabilities

The Commission is able to make modest grants to help with the organisation of **sports events** with a European dimension, and involving participants with disabilities from the majority of EC countries. In 1991, for example, the Highland Sports Association received support for their open day. In 1992 there was only about £100 000 available for this work. Typically **grants fall into the range £1 500 to £15 000**. They should be used to promote sport as an activity for people with disabilities. They should also increase public awareness of the European Community and of the talents of people with disabilities.

Criteria and procedures

Size of grants

Applications can be made at any time up to 1st September in the year prior to the year of the event. Applications should be made to the British Paralympic Association, which acts as the secretariat to the National Committee. The project must originate from a legal body or organisation, be open to participation from at least four EC countries, preferably be of an innovatory nature and must include an indication of how the Community's support will be made known. The application should include background, justification, aims and objectives, a statement of benefits to be achieved, the disability group(s) involved, number of participants and a budget.

British Paralympic Association, Room G13A, Delta Point, 35 Wellesley Road, Croydon, Surrey CR9 2YZ. Tel: 081 666 4556, Fax: 081 666 4617

European Parliament special budget provision

Very occasionally the European Parliament will make a special budget provision for a particularly important event. For example, the 1992 Paralympics were voted about £700 000. This sort of arrangement is achieved by lobbying the Parliament rather than by applying to the Commission (see Chapter 3).

9-4
Elderly People

1993 European Year

1993 is the **"European Year of Older People and Solidarity between Generations"**. This is seen as an occasion for celebration and for reflection. The Commission will be providing some financial support for studies, conferences and seminars on topics concerning older people and their interaction with all other sections of society.

Criteria for support

It would be willing to consider providing support for events, including sports-related activities, which meet the following requirements:
• activities must have a strong "European" dimension – involving people from a number of European Community countries;
• funding will focus on activities which improve awareness and understanding amongst the general public on questions of concern to older people.

Funding from the Commission will never cover more than 60% of the costs of the event, Preference will be given to activities involving large numbers of people during 1993 and which involve different generations working together.

Applications should be made to:
Eamon McInerney, Commission of the European Communities, Office C-80 2/20, 200 Rue de la Loi, 1049 Brussels, Belgium Tel: 010 32 2 299 0494, Fax: 010 32 2 299 0509 or to the UK European Year 1993 Secretariat - Amanda Bennett, c/o Age Concern, 1268 London Road, London SW16 4ER. Tel: 081 679 8000, Fax: 081 679 6069

9-5
TIDE

TIDE is the European Community's action programme for **technology and development** in aid of the integration of elderly people and people facing disabilities. It is possible to envisage support from TIDE for a project which used some relevant technology to enable people to take a full part in sporting life, though such an application has yet to be submitted.

Applications are made in response to occasional calls for tender. For full information contact:
Mr Egidio Ballabio, DG XIII/C/3, Commission of the European Communities, 200 Rue de la Loi, 1049 Brussels, Belgium
Tel: 010 32 2 299 0240, Fax: 010 32 2 299 0248

9-6

Community Assistance for Organisations of or for Migrants

For this purpose, the European Community uses the expression "migrant" to mean anyone who has taken up residence in a different Community country, anyone of foreign origin belonging to an ethnic minority or any recognised refugee. Grants are available to assist in projects aimed at the integration of **migrant workers** and their families. In the sports context, this may include measures which opened sporting opportunities to black people.

Grants are one-off and are typically of about £6 000 though they can range from **£2 000 to an absolute maximum of £15 000**. Applications are made direct to the Commission on forms available from the address below. It takes about four months before a decision is reached. For full information contact:
Ms Annette Bosscher, DG V/C/2, Commission of the European Communities, 200 Rue de la Loi, 1049 Brussels, Belgium
Tel: 010 32 2 295 1052, Fax: 010 32 2 295 0129

Size of grants

Application procedure

9-7

Local Employment Initiatives by Women

The Commission has about £1 million available each year to provide **small grants for women setting up businesses**. This could include women's sports organisations provided that management positions and the majority of jobs are held by women (see box page 68). There is no restriction on the legal form of the enterprise nor on the activity to be carried out.

Budget available for women's businesses

Grants are small, about £1 000 for each full-time job created for a woman, with a minimum of two and a maximum of five jobs. They are allocated taking into account the financial viability of the project and also the extent to which particularly deprived groups of women will benefit from the jobs. Proof of the employment having started will be needed. Applications are made on a standard form. They need to be submitted to both the addresses shown. Applications must be submitted before the starting date of the project.

Criteria and procedures

Application forms, further information and advice are available from:
Dr Patricia Richardson, Women's Enterprise Unit, SEF, University of Stirling,
Stirling FK9 4LA. Tel: 0786 67353/67348, Fax: 0786 50201 or from
Women's LEI Grants Management, Comitato Impresa Donna – CNA,
1 Avenue de la Joyeuse Entrée, 1040 Brussels, Belgium
Tel: 010 32 2 280 0054/0992, Fax: 010 32 2 280 0901

Islay and Jura Community Enterprise

After more than ten years of hard work by a predominantly female committee, this community company was able to open the first public swimming pool on the island of Islay, providing a much needed community resource. The pool is in a redundant warehouse made available by the local whisky distillery, which also provides its waste heat to cut the running costs of the pool.

The pool provides employment for four workers, three of them, including two leisure assistants, being female. A grant from the European Community's Local Employment Initiatives Programme towards the cost of providing these jobs was one of the sources of income for the company.

The main problem they faced in connection with this grant was in finding out about the programme in the first place. Islay and Jura Community Enterprise had considered many other ways of raising money from the EC without being aware that this scheme was available until their Regional Councillor mentioned the possibility. After that actually making the application was straightforward and the money came through reasonably quickly.

9-8
Combating Drug Abuse

Support for projects to combat drug abuse

The Commission has a major programme of public health activities. These include work in connection with AIDS, alcohol and the fight against drug abuse. Work on drug abuse includes the drafting of a **code of conduct in the field of drugs in sport** and a health education campaign to reduce the extent of drug use in general. Sports organisations could ask for financial support for projects in either area. This is a relatively new scheme and there are, as yet, no indications of a typical size for a grant.

Criteria and procedures

Applications are best made at the beginning of the year and must be made at least six months in advance. They should cover more than one European Community country, though it is possible for grants to be made for activities carried out in only one country if they are supported by, or inspired by, projects in other countries. Emphasis is placed on clear plans for evaluation and dissemination. Applicants should contact:
Division V/E/1 – Public Health, Commission of the European Communities,
2920 Luxembourg
Tel: 010 352 4301 2737, Fax: 010 352 4301 4511

Chapter **10**

Helping sports organisations in developing countries

European Development Fund

The European Community has a tradition of aid to the countries of the South which dates back to the earliest days of the Community. The first **European Development Fund** was established in 1958 and covered 19 African countries, many of them French colonies at the time. The latest (seventh) European Development Fund was established under the terms of a Convention signed in Lomé in 1989 between the 12 European Community countries and the 69 "ACP" countries (see box below for a list). In addition, the European Community has separate arrangements for working with Latin American, Asian and Mediterranean countries.

Development aid

In total these programmes were expected to spend well **over 2 billion (2 000 000 000) pounds in 1992.** The money is, to a very large extent, allocated at the level of the developing country concerned. Sports organisations wishing to help their counterparts in such countries should urge them to contact the local representative of the Commission. However, in addition to these programmes, the Commission spends some £250 million on other development aid programmes. In the Commission, most of the administration of these schemes is undertaken by Directorate-General VIII (Development), but in a few cases it is Directorate-General I (External Affairs) that carries out the work.

The ACP States

Angola	Gambia	St Kitts and Nevis
Antigua & Barbuda	Ghana	St Lucia
Bahamas	Grenada	St Vincent and the Grenadines
Barbados	Guinea	
Belize	Guinea-Bissau	Sao Tome & Principe
Benin	Guyana	Senegal
Botswana	Haiti	Seychelles
Burkina Faso	Jamaica	Sierra Leone
Burundi	Kenya	Solomon Islands
Cameroon	Kiribati	Somalia
Cape Verde	Lesotho	Sudan
Central African Republic	Liberia	Surinam
Chad	Madagascar	Swaziland
Comoros	Malawi	Tanzania
Congo	Mali	Togo
Côte d'Ivoire	Mauritania	Tonga
Djibouti	Mauritius	Trinidad & Tobago
Dominica	Mozambique	Tuvalu
Dominican Republic	Namibia	Uganda
Equatorial Guinea	Niger	Western Samoa
Ethiopia	Nigeria	Vanuatu
Fiji	Papua New Guinea	Zaire
Gabon	Rwanda	Zambia
		Zimbabwe

10-1

Support for development projects in developing countries co-financed by non-governmental organisations

The Commission has considerable funds (about £80 million in 1992) which are made available to non-governmental organisations in the EC countries who use them to match their contribution to development programmes in developing countries. This is the most conspicuous aspect of a wide-ranging and close relationship between the Commission and non-governmental organisations concerned with development questions. The Commission provides support for a Liaison Committee which channels the views of the organisations to the Commission (see box page 72).

Joint NGO ventures

To be eligible for Commission co-financing, projects should be based on the wishes of the benefiting community. They must be sound economic and social ventures, capable of continuing after the external aid has ceased. They should be acceptable to the authorities of the country concerned. **Grants can be up to about £100 000 a year and can run for a maximum of five years**.

For full advice and information contact:
Bernard Ryelandt, Division VIII/B/2, Commission of the European Communities, 200 Rue de la Loi, 1049 Brussels, Belgium Tel: 010 32 2 299 9861, Fax: 010 32 2 299 2847

10-2

Programme to Control the Spread of AIDS

In 1992 the Commission's Aids Task Force had a total of 61 projects for AIDS prevention under implementation in 52 countries in Africa, Asia and Latin America, with a further 18 projects under preparation. These projects were mainly aimed at supporting AIDS awareness and behavioural change targeted at groups at risk of AIDS infection, control and prevention of sexually transmitted diseases and blood safety.

AIDS awareness

The AIDS prevention activities funded by the Commission have not, so far, been specifically connected with sports organisations. It is recognised though that sporting events can be important for passing AIDS prevention messages aimed at the general public and that collaboration with sports organisations from Europe with partners in developing countries could make a contribution.

For full details contact:
Dr L Fransen, Aids Task Force, 67A Rue Joseph II, 1040 Brussels, Belgium Tel: 010 32 2 231 1495, Fax: 010 32 2 230 5671

The Liaison Committee of Development NGOs to the European Community

Non-governmental organisations (NGOs) have had an important role in the development work of the European Community since the earliest days. For the last twenty years their contribution has been recognised by a consultative structure. In its present form this "Liaison Committee" has twelve national members – one from each EC country – and five specialists, who chair working groups in their subject. The national members are elected by national networks which bring together all the relevant organisations in the country concerned. These national networks also elect representative members to attend annual assemblies which allow discussion on topics of interest to both the NGOs and the Commission.

Membership of a national network is not essential for applications for funding, which are handled directly by the Commission. It is, however, an important channel for information and influence.

The Liaison Committee is serviced by a small Secretariat:
Liaison Committee of Development NGOs to the EC, 62 Avenue de Cortenbergh, 1040 Brussels, Belgium
Tel: 010 32 2 736 4087, Fax: 010 32 2 732 1934

10-3

Campaign against Drug Abuse

The European Community runs a substantial (£7 million in 1992) programme of activities in connection with international efforts to control drug abuse. Some of this is available for seminars, research and awareness campaigns in developing countries and sports organisations may feel that they have a contribution to make. Successful applications can be funded up to 85% of the cost of the project. For full details contact:
Mr Robert Medeiros, Directorate-General I/K/2, Commission of the European Communities, 200 Rue de la Loi, 1049 Brussels, Belgium
Tel: 010 32 2 299 2321, Fax: 010 32 2 299 0914

10-4

Technical Co-operation with Latin America

The Commission has programmes of technical co-operation with most of the non-ACP developing countries. The allocation for Latin American countries has specific provision for transfers of knowledge in the cultural field on the basis of European organisations working in this field. This would cover the transfer of European experience of the development of infrastructure or the tourist industry linked to sporting events, for example. Contact:
Mr Anacoreta Correia, Directorate-General I/I, Commission of the European Communities, 200 Rue de la Loi, 1049 Brussels, Belgium
Tel: 010 32 2 299 3251, Fax: 010 32 2 299 2897

Chapter **11**

Sources of further information

**Direct contact
with Brussels**

Interested parties should not be afraid to write, telephone or fax Commission officials in Brussels. It is important to realise that Commission officials are able to be much more open than their Whitehall counterparts. Most of the other Brussels agencies have a contract with the Commission to provide information to the public and are equally helpful.

Further information can be obtained from the offices of the Commission (see box below). The London office has a comprehensive set of European Community documentation which can be consulted between 10am and 1pm on working days. In the afternoons they deal with telephone questions. The box below also gives the address of the London office of the European Parliament which offers a full and very helpful service of information about the work of the Parliament. It is open 10am – 1pm and 2pm – 5pm on Mondays to Thursdays.

**The UK offices of the
Commission are at:**

8 Storey's Gate
London SW1P 3AT
Tel: 071 973 1992
Fax: 071 973 1900

4 Cathedral Road
Cardiff CF1 9SG
Tel: 0222 371631
Fax: 0222 395489

9 Alva Street
Edinburgh EH2 4PH
Tel: 031 225 2058
Fax: 031 226 4105

9-15 Bedford Street
Belfast BT2 7EG
Tel: 0232 240708
Fax: 0232 248241

**and the London office of the
Parliament is at:**

2 Queen Anne's Gate
London SW1H 9AA
Tel: 071 222 0411
Fax: 071 222 2713

**Official Journal
of the European
Communities**

The key texts likely to be needed are the **"Official Journal"**, which incorporates a record of all the legislation that the Council enacts, a record of the workings of the Parliament and a notice board for announcements and tenders, and **"COM" documents**, each of which contain a Commission proposal or report. The formal proposals also appear in the 'Official Journal', but in a COM document they are accompanied by an explanatory memorandum.

These documents can all be consulted at the Commission offices. They are also available at **"European Documentation Centres"** which are based in 50 UK libraries, mainly in universities (see box opposite for a list).

**Other
Community
documentation**

Frustratingly, in recent years the Commission has been tending to issue consultation documents in the form of **"SEC" documents**. SEC documents were originally meant to be for the internal use of the Commission only and there is no reliable method of obtaining them. If you know one exists, your

European Documentation Centres in the United Kingdom

ABERDEEN
The University
0204 272000 x2587

ASHFORD, Kent
Wye College
0223 812401 x497

BATH
The University
0225 826826 x5594

BELFAST
Queens University
0232 245133 x3605

BIRMINGHAM
The University
021 414 5823
and
The University of Central England
021 331 5298

BRADFORD
The University
0274 383402

BRIGHTON
University of Sussex
0273 678159

BRISTOL
The University
0272 303370

CAMBRIDGE
The University Library
0233 333138

CANTERBURY
University of Kent
0227 764000 x3109

CARDIFF
The University
0222 874262

COLCHESTER
University of Essex
0206 873333 x3181

COLERAINE
University of Ulster
0265 44141 x4257

COVENTRY
Coventry University
0203 838452
and
University of Warwick
0203 523523 x2041

DUNDEE
The University
0382 23181 x4100

DURHAM
The University
091 374 3041

EDINBURGH
The University
031 667 1011 x4292

EXETER
The University
0392 263356

GLASGOW
The University
041 339 8855 x6744

GUILDFORD
University of Surrey
0483 509233

HULL
The University
0482 465940

KEELE
The University
0782 621111 x3738

LANCASTER
The University
0524 65201 x2543

LEEDS
Leeds University
0532 335040
and
Leeds Metropolitan University
0532 832600 x3280

LEICESTER
The University
0533 522044

LONDON
Queen Mary & Westfield College
071 975 5555 x3327
and
The University of North London
071 607 2789 x4110
and
Royal Institute of International
Affairs
071 930 2233 x260
and

continued overleaf

European Documentation Centres in the United Kingdom

continued from page 75
London School of Economics
071 955 7273

LOUGHBOROUGH
The University
0509 222344

MANCHESTER
The University
061 275 3751

NEWCASTLE UPON TYNE
The University
091 232 6002 x4136

NORWICH
University of East Anglia
0603 56161 x2412

NOTTINGHAM
The University
0602 484848 x3741

OXFORD
Bodleian Library
0865 277201

PORTSMOUTH
The University
0705 827681

READING
The University
0734 318782

SALFORD
The University
061 736 5843 x7209

SHEFFIELD
Sheffield Hallam University
0742 532126

SOUTHAMPTON
The University
0703 595000

WOLVERHAMPTON
The University
0902 313005 x2300

best bet is to ask the Commission official concerned to send you a copy. A good example is SEC(91) 1438, which deals with EC policies in the field of sport. Copies of this are available from:

Division X/C/4, Commission of the European Communities, 200 Rue de la Loi, 1049 Brussels, Belgium
Tel: 010 32 2 299 9421, Fax: 010 32 2 299 9284

The most frustrating thing, however, is that there is no routine means of finding out which SEC documents exist.

It is possible to subscribe to the Official Journal and to the COM series. Her Majesty's Stationery Office is the main UK agent for all official EC publications. It can be contacted at:

HMSO Publications, 51 Nine Elms Lane, London SW8 5DR
Tel: 071 873 8409, Fax: 071 873 8463

Separate issues can also be bought. For example, the budget of the Communities appears as an issue of the Official Journal – often in February.

General publications

For a good general view of what is going on in the European Community, you should ask the London office of the Commission to put you on the mailing list for their information sheet **'The Week in Europe'**. This is produced mainly for journalists and gives, on two sides of A4, a paragraph about the key events of the previous week. The Commission offices also have a wide range of other

Useful Books

European Community – the Building of a Union   John Pinder
Oxford University Press, Oxford, 1991

This sets the present political discussions in their historical context.

★ ★ ★

The Happy European – a Survival Guide to the EC   Laetitia de Warren
Charles Letts, London, 1992

and

The European Community – a Guide to the Maze   Stanley A Budd
Kogan Page, London   and Alun Jones

Two sources of general information. Of the two the first is more readable and the second contains more hard information. Budd & Jones is revised often and you should look for the latest edition.

★ ★ ★

Networking in Europe   Brian Harvey
NCVO Publications and CDF, London, 1992

A comprehensive and readable guide to the subject of getting in touch with others. Written for voluntary organisations.

★ ★ ★

A Rough Guide to Europe – Local Authorities and the EC   Audit Commission
HMSO, London, 1991

In 97 paragraphs, this book shows a local authority the key considerations in deciding what to do about the EC. The approach and much of the material is very relevant to other organisations.

★ ★ ★

Grants from Europe – How to Get Money and   Ann Davison
Influence Policy   and Bill Seary
NCVO Publications, London

The standard text on the subject for voluntary organisations. Check that you get the latest edition.

★ ★ ★

1992 Eurospeak Explained   Stephen Crampton
Rosters, London

A jargon-busting glossary.

★ ★ ★

EC Research Funding   Lieselotte Krickau-Richter
Commission of the European   and Otto von Schwerin
Communities
3rd Edition 1992

The Commission's own, comprehensive guide for applicants.

material, much of it free. Of particular interest are **'Finance from Europe – a guide to grants and loans from the European Community'** and **'European File 2/1992 – The European Community and Sport'**.

More detailed information is supplied by two monthly bulletins:
- The Euro-Citizen Action Service (ECAS) publishes **'The European Citizen'** which contains articles and listings of interest to non-profit organisations. Contact:
  ECAS, 1 Rue de Facyz, 1050 Brussels, Belgium
  Tel: 010 32 2 512 9360, Fax: 010 32 2 512 6673
- The Local Government International Bureau (LGIB) publication **'European Information Service'** which appears ten times a year. It is a comprehensive guide to matters of interest to local authorities and covers most of the subjects that would interest sports organisations. For subscription details contact:
  LGIB, 35 Great Smith Street, London SW1P 3BJ
  Tel: 071 222 1636, Fax: 071 233 2179

A different sort of periodical is **'Vacher's European Companion'**. This appears quarterly and supplies up-to-date details of Commission officials, MEPs, government representatives and many of the other actors on the Community stage. It can be bought either on subscription or as single issues. Contact:
Vachers Publications, 113 High Street, Berkhamsted, Herts HP4 2DJ
Tel: 0442 876135

There are now many books about the European Community. A selection of particularly useful ones is given in the box page 77.

Sports Council International Affairs Unit

For more individual advice and information sports organisations should contact:
International Affairs Unit, The Sports Council, Walkden House,
3-10 Melton Street, London NW1 2EB
Tel: 071 383 3896, Fax: 071 383 3147

Chapter 12

Sport and European organisations

The aim of this chapter is to give an outline of four additional institutions with a sporting interest, namely the Council of Europe, the Association of European National Olympic Committees (AENOC), the European Non-Governmental Sports Organisation (ENGSO), the European Sports Conference (ESC), and also one further international organisation, the General Association of International Sports Federations (GAISF).

12-1
Council of Europe

Council of Europe

The Council of Europe, the **European cultural inter-governmental institution**, comprises all democratic European countries (see Appendix 8). Historically, it was the non-federalist European institution which emphasised voluntary co-operation in areas of mutual interest amongst its members.

Situated in Strasbourg and, somewhat confusingly, sharing a site with the European Parliament of the EC when in session, it is best known for its **Human Rights Convention** and the **European Court of Human Rights**. It also does useful work in a number of areas such as the environment, education and local government.

The Council of Europe has a directorate with sole responsibility for sport. Through this directorate, the **European Ministers responsible for sport meet every three years** to draw up guidelines for the Council of Europe's sports policy and to discuss problems arising in international sport. They also hold **informal European Ministers meetings** within the three year cycle, if required.

CDDS

The **Steering Committee for the Development of Sport (CDDS)**, consisting of national governmental and non-governmental officials, prepares and implements the ministers' decisions. It decides the annual work programme and organises seminars and workshops on sports-related issues. It meets annually in February/March.

Expert Committees

The CDDS is assisted in its work by the Committee of Experts on **Sports Research** and by the Committee of Experts on **Sports Information**. The Sports Research Committee co-ordinates research projects and monitors documentation and information on sports research through a European sports databank. This information is sent to a specialised information centre, the **Clearing House** set up in Brussels in 1972 and sponsored by the Council of Europe. Information is analysed at regular intervals and circulated to the countries which take part in the Council of Europe's activities in the field of sport in a **Sports Information Bulletin** issued four times a year.

Two full Conventions, the Convention on Anti-Doping and the Convention on Spectator Violence at Sports Events provide for close co-operation between Member States. Monitoring groups closely follow the implementation of the Conventions in Member States.

The Committee for the Development of Sport (CDDS) recently completed a project on sports injuries and their prevention, and is involved in projects on the Economic Impact of Sport, Ethics in Sport and Young People, and the writing of a new European Sports Charter. The CDDS is also involved in training programmes in sports administration in Central and Eastern Europe.

The UK delegation to the CDDS Annual Steering Committee meeting comprises representation from the Sports Council, the Sport and Recreation Division of the Department of National Heritage (SARD) and the British Sports Forum.

Anti-Doping and Spectator Violence Conventions

Specific sports projects

12-2
European Non-Governmental Sports Organisation (ENGSO)

The European Non-Governmental Sports Organisation (ENGSO) was **formerly the NGO Club**. It was established in the early 70s as a club of professional Secretaries-General of European national sports confederations or their representatives around the time when the Council of Europe was becoming more involved in sport.

ENGSO

In 1990 the name was changed to ENGSO in order to reflect more properly the changing role of the organisation. Slightly amended aims and objectives were adopted in the light of recent political developments in Europe. Certain Central and Eastern European nation states which have established sports confederations have been admitted to membership.

Terms of reference

According to the ENGSO terms of reference, established in **Liechtenstein** in 1990, "the aim of ENGSO is to improve sport in the member countries by:
• sharing information on national sports development;
• discussing current sports political issues;
• seeking common positions on sports issues, and by 'marketing these positions'."

The organisation also has a permanent **EC Working Group** which monitors developments as they affect sport.

EC Working Group

At each full ENGSO meeting, member countries submit a written **'Country Report'** detailing the most important recent sports developments. The Central Council of Physical Recreation (CCPR) represents the UK on ENGSO. Meetings take place twice a year.

Country Report

12-3

Association of European National Olympic Committees (AENOC)

AENOC

The aims of the Association of European National Olympic Committees (AENOC) are to further the Olympic ideals throughout Europe, including the education of youth through sport, the promotion of **co-operation between individual European National Olympic Committees** (NOCs) through research, study and the exchange of information and also the development in Europe of "Olympic Solidarity" programmes in collaboration with the IOC.

Permanent commissions

Since the middle of 1991, AENOC has seen its membership rise from 33 to **45 NOCs** and will probably have 47 members by the end of 1992. The organisation has permanent commissions on the preparation of the Olympic Games, marketing, finance, technical co-operation, medical and scientific matters, legal affairs and press and communications. AENOC organises **seminars** for Secretaries-General and Chefs de Mission on a wide range of issues. In close collaboration with the IOC, it is also currently supporting the new NOCs, not only with limited help in hard currency but also in the training of new administrators.

AENOC has also established a **liaison office with the EC** in Brussels and where necessary acts as a lobbying group for the Olympic movement both in respect of the EC and also the Council of Europe. In 1990 AENOC created the European Youth Olympic Days (EYOD). The first summer Games were held in Brussels in 1991. Two thousand five hundred European athletes participated in those games in ten Olympic sports. The EYOD summer and winter Games will be organised every two years. AENOC also publishes a magazine **'Sporteurope'**.

The British Olympic Association is the official UK representation.

12-4

European Sports Conference (ESC)

ESC

The European Sports Conference was born of the Ostpolitik phase of the Cold War in the early 70s. It meets every two years in a different country. Hitherto, the Conference provided a **forum** for sports administrators from **both East and West Europe** to discuss issues of mutual interest. Whilst each Conference has had a specific theme, considerable emphasis was always given to the unofficial bilateral negotiations between Member States which took place during the Conference.

Working Groups

In recent years, the ESC has instituted a number of **Working Groups**. One Group established a European Sports Charter; other subjects have included anti-doping strategies and scientific work and co-operation. There are currently four Working Groups examining the issues of Women and Sport, Europe's Position in the World, Youth, and East-West Co-operation within Europe respectively. The ESC has no permanent secretariat. Appropriate administrative support is provided by the organising country of the next Conference.

The Sports Council is currently the lead UK body for the ESC. The **next Conference** will be held in **Bratislava** in September 1993, with the theme **"Changing Europe – Changing Sport"**.

Bratislava Conference

12-5

General Association of International Sports Federations (GAISF)

The General Association of International Sports Federations **represents the worldwide interests of international sports federations**.

GAISF

Amongst the objectives laid down in its statutes, GAISF:

Objectives

- maintains the authority and autonomy of its members;
- promotes closer links with its members and all other sports organisations;
- co-ordinates and protects common interest;
- collects, verifies and disseminates information.

In a formal declaration in 1983, a text was approved which expresses the international sports movement's will to preserve sport's fundamental values and most particularly its educational aspects despite the strong pressure with which it is presently confronted.

Every year an annual **GAISF Congress** is held on a specific subject. The role of international federations in the Olympic movement, women and sport, and the media have been subjects of recent conferences.

Annual Congress

GAISF News is the **monthly bulletin** of the organisation. The **GAISF calendar** is published twice a year which compiles the dates of the international competitions and championships officially recognised by the GAISF members, a general chronological calendar for the coming six months and a long-term calendar planned by each international federation and a list of future congresses.

Publications

The permanent headquarters and administration secretariat have been located in Monte Carlo since 1977.

Appendices

Appendix 1   **Staff Structure of the Commission of the European Communities**

Secretariat-General

Legal Service

Spokesman's Service

Interpretation and Conference Service

Statistical Office

Consumer Policy Service

Task Force for Human Resources, Education, Training and Youth

Directorate-General I	External relations
Directorate-General II	Economic and Financial Affairs
Directorate-General III	Internal Market and Industrial Affairs
Directorate-General IV	Competition
Directorate-General V	Employment, Industrial Relations and Social Affairs
Directorate-General VI	Agriculture
Directorate-General VII	Transport
Directorate-General VIII	Development
Directorate-General IX	Personnel and Administration
Directorate-General X	Audiovisual, Information, Communication and Culture
Directorate-General XI	Environment, Nuclear Safety and Civil Protection
Directorate-General XII	Science, Research and Development
Directorate-General XIII	Telecommunications, Information Industries and Innovation
Directorate-General XIV	Fisheries
Directorate-General XV	Financial Institutions and Company Law
Directorate-General XVI	Regional Policies
Directorate-General XVII	Energy
Directorate-General XVIII	Credit and Investments
Directorate-General XIX	Budgets
Directorate-General XX	Financial Control
Directorate-General XXI	Customs and Indirect Taxation
Directorate-General XXII	Enterprise Policy, Distributive Trades, Tourism and Co-operatives

United Kingdom Members of the European Parliament   Appendix 2

Bedfordshire South
Mr Peter Beazley
Rest Harrow
14 The Combe
Ratton
Eastbourne
E. Sussex BN20 9DB
Tel: 0323 504460

Birmingham East
Mrs Christine Crawley
16 Bristol Street
Birmingham B5 7AA
Tel: 021 622 2270
Fax: 021 666 7332

Birmingham West
Mr John Tomlinson
42 Bridge Street
Walsall WS1 1JQ
Tel: 0922 22586
Fax: 0922 724923

Bristol
Mr Ian White
138 Gloucester Rd. North
Filton
Bristol BS12 7BQ
Tel: 0272 236933
Fax: 0272 236966

**Cambridgeshire
and Bedfordshire
North**
Sir Fred Catherwood
Shire Hall
Castle Hill
Cambridge CB3 0AW
Tel: 0223 317672
Fax: 0223 317671

Cheshire East
Mr Brian Simpson
Gilbert Kakefield House
67 Bewsey Street
Warrington WA2 7JQ
Tel: 0925 728093
Fax: 0925 240799

Cheshire West
Mr Lyndon Harrison
2 Stanley Street
Chester CH1 2LR
Tel: 0244 320623
Fax: 0244 350355

**Cleveland &
Yorkshire North**
Mr David Bowe
10 Harris Street
Middlesbrough TS1 5EF
Tel: 0642 247722
Fax: 0642 247804

**Cornwall and
Plymouth**
Mr Christopher Beazley
The Grange
Devoran
Truro
Cornwall TR3 6PF
Tel: 0872 862132
Fax: 0872 865917

Cotswolds
Lord Plumb
Maxstoke
Coleshill
Warwickshire B46 2QJ
Tel: 0675 463133
Fax: 0675 464156

**Cumbria and
Lancashire North**
Lord Inglewood
Hutton in the Forest
Penrith
Cumbria CA11 9TH
Tel: 0853 4500
Fax: 0853 4571

Derbyshire
Mr Geoffrey Hoon
8 Station Street
Kirkby-in-Ashfield
Nottinghamshire
NG17 7AR
Tel: 0623 720399
Fax: 0332 295818

Devon
Lord O'Hagan
12 Lyndhurst Road
Exeter
Devon EX2 4PA
Tel: 0392 410532
Fax: 0392 413427

**Dorset East and
Hampshire West**
Mr Bryan Cassidy
The Stables
White Cliff Gardens
Blandford Forum
Dorset DT11 7BU
Tel: 0258 452420
Fax: 071 937 3558

Durham
Mr Stephen Hughes
County Hall, Room 4/74
Durham DH1 5UR
Tel: 091 384 9371
Fax: 091 384 6100

Essex North East
Miss Anne McIntosh
The Old Armoury
Museum Street
Saffron Walden
Essex CB10 1JN
Tel: 0799 23631
Fax: 0799 23631

Essex South West
Miss Patricia Rawlings
122 The Stow
Harlow
Essex CM20 3AS
Tel: 0279 429251
Fax: 0279 434788

**Greater Manchester
Central**
Mr Edward Newman
7th Floor Graeme House
Wilbraham Road
Chorlton cum Hardy
Manchester M21 1AQ
Tel: 061 881 2144

**Greater Manchester
East**
Mr Glyn Ford
46 Stamford Road
Mossley
Lancashire OL5 0BE
Tel: 0457 836276
Fax: 0457 834927

Greater Manchester West
Mr Gary Titley
16 Spring Lane
Radcliffe M26 9TQ
Tel: 061 724 4008
Fax: 061 724 4009

Hampshire Central
Mr E. Kellett-Bowman
4A Desborough Road
Eastleigh
Hampshire SO5 5NX
Tel: 0703 617219
Fax: 0256 763333

Hereford and Worcester
Sir James Scott-Hopkins
Bicknor House
English Bicknor, Coleford
Gloucester GL16 7PF
Tel: 0594 60234
Fax: 071 219 4898

Hertfordshire
Mr Derek Prag
Pine Hill
47 New Road
Digswell
Welwyn
Herts AL6 0AQ
Tel: 0438 712999
Fax: 0438 840422

Humberside
Mr Peter Crampton
135 Westbourne Avenue
Hull HU5 3HU
Tel: 0482 449337
Fax: 0482 449403

Kent East
Mr Christopher Jackson
8 Wellmeade Drive
Sevenoaks
Kent TN13 1QA
Tel: 0732 456688
Fax: 0732 741117

Kent West
Mr Ben Patterson
Elm Hill House
Hawkhurst, Cranbrook
Kent TN18 4XU
Tel: 0580 753260
Fax: 0580 753260

Lancashire Central
Mr Michael Welsh
Watercrook
181 Town Lane
Whittle-le-Woods
Chorley
Lancs PR6 8AG
Tel: 0257 276992
Fax: 0257 231254

Lancashire East
Mr Michael Hindley
ELCA Research
Old Municipal Offices
Bury Road
Haslingden BB4 5PG
Tel: 0706 830013
Fax: 0706 830536

Leeds
Mr Michael McGowan
Civic Hall
Leeds LS1 1UR
Tel: 0943 462864

Leicester
Mrs Mel Read
81 Great Central Street
Leicester LE1 4ND
Tel: 0533 532035
Fax: 0533 532038

Lincolnshire
Mr William Newton Dunn
10 Church Lane
Navenby
Lincs LN5 0EG
Tel: 0522 810812

London Central
Mr Stan Newens
The Leys
18 Park Hill, Harlow
Essex CM17 0AE
Tel: 0279 420108
Fax: 071 792 3691

London East
Ms Carole Tongue
97A Ilford Lane, Ilford
Tel: 081 514 0198
Fax: 081 553 4764

London North
Mrs Pauline Green
800 High Road
Tottenham
London N17 0DH
Tel: 081 449 4885
Fax: 081 365 1894

London North East
Mr Alf Lomas
Site 2, 2nd Floor
78/102 The Broadway
Stratford
London E15 1NL
Tel: 081 519 8114
Fax: 081 503 0028

London North West
Lord Bethell
73 Sussex Square
London W2 2SS
Tel: 071 402 6877
Fax: 071 706 1287

London South and Surrey East
Mr James Moorhouse
34 Buckingham Palace
Road, London SW1W 0RE
Tel: 071 828 3153
Fax: 071 630 9750

London South East
Mr Peter Price
60 Marlings Park Avenue
Chislehurst
Kent BR7 6RD
Tel: 0689 820681
Fax: 0689 890622

London South Inner
Mr Richard Balfe
132 Powis Street
London SE18 6NL
Tel: 081 855 2128
Fax: 081 316 1936

London South West
Mrs Anita Pollack
177 Lavender Hill
London SW11 5TE
Tel: 071 228 0839
Fax: 071 228 0916

London West
Mr Michael Elliott
358 Oldfield Lane North
Greenford
Middlesex UB6 8PT
Tel: 081 578 1303

Merseyside East
Mr Terry Wynn
105 Corporation Street
St Helens
Merseyside WA10 1SX
Tel: 0744 451609
Fax: 0744 29832

Merseyside West
Mr Kenneth Stewart
62 Ballantyne Road
Liverpool L13 9AL
Tel: 051 256 7782

Midlands Central
Ms Christine Oddy
3 Copthall House
Station Square
Coventry CV1 2FZ
Tel: 0203 552328
Fax: 0203 551424

Midlands West
Mr John Bird
Rooms 2/3 Gresham
Chambers,
14 Lichfield Street
Wolverhampton WV1 1DP
Tel: 0902 20276
Fax: 0902 20276

Norfolk
Mr Paul Howell
The White House Farm
Bradenham Road
Scarning, East Dereham
Norfolk NR20 3EY
Tel: 0362 87239
Fax: 0362 87536

Northamptonshire
Mr Anthony Simpson
Bassets, Great Glen
Leicestershire LE8 0GQ
Tel: 0537 592386

Northumbria
Mr Gordon Adam
10 Coach Road, Wallsend
Tyne & Wear NE26 6JA
Tel: 091 263 5838
Fax: 091 263 7079

Nottingham
Mr Kenneth Coates
112 Church Street
Matlock DE4 3BZ
Tel: 0629 57159
Fax: 0629 580672

Oxford and Buckinghamshire
Mr James Elles
Conservative Centre
Church Street, Amersham
Bucks HP7 0DB
Tel: 0494 721577
Fax: 0494 722107

Sheffield
Mr Roger Barton
54 Pinestone Street
Sheffield S1 2HN
Tel: 0742 753431
Fax: 0742 739666

Shropshire and Stafford
Sir Christopher Prout
5 Oakfield Road
Shrewsbury
Shropshire SY3 8AA
Tel: 0630 83218
Fax: 071 222 2501

Somerset and Dorset West
Mrs Margaret Daly
The Old School House
Aisholt,
Spaxton, Bridgwater
Somerset TA5 1AR
Tel: 0278 67688
Fax: 0278 67684

Staffordshire East
Mr George Stevenson
76/80 Lonsdale Street
Stoke on Trent ST4 4DP
Tel: 0782 414232
Fax: 0782 744785

Suffolk
Mr Amedee Turner
The Barn,
Westleton
Saxmundham
Suffolk IP17 3AN
Tel: 0728 73235
Fax: 071 235 9237

Surrey West
Mr Tom Spencer
Thornfalcon House
Northchapel
West Sussex GU28 9HP
Tel: 0428 78756
Fax: 0428 78401

Sussex East
Sir Jack Stewart-Clark
Puckstye House
Holtye Common
Cowden
Kent TN8 7EL
Tel: 0342 850285
Fax: 0342 850789

Sussex West
Mr Madron Seligman
Micklepage House
Nuthurst, Horsham
West Sussex RH13 6RG
Tel: 0403 891533
Fax: 0403 891010

Thames Valley
Mr John Stevens
15 St James's Place
London SW1A 1NW
Tel: 071 493 8111
Fax: 071 493 0673

Tyne and Wear
Mr Alan Donnelly
1 South View, Jarrow
Tel: 091 489 7643

Wight and Hampshire East
Mr Richard Simmonds
Woodlands Farm
Cookham Dean
Maidenhead
Berkshire SL6 9PL
Tel: 0628 44684
Fax: 0628 898128

Wiltshire
Mrs Caroline Jackson
New House, Hanney Road
Southmoor, Abingdon
Oxon OX13 5HR
Tel: 0865 821243
Fax: 071 233 5344

York
Mr E. McMillan-Scott
109 Town Street
Old Malton
North Yorkshire
YO17 0HD
Tel: 0653 693277
Fax: 0653 696108

Yorkshire South
Mr Norman West
43 Coronation Drive
Birdwell
Barnsley S10 5RJ
Tel: 0226 287464

Yorkshire South West
Mr Tom Megahy
3 Burton Street
Wakefield
West Yorkshire WF1 2DD
Tel: 0924 382396
Fax: 0924 366851

Yorkshire West
Mr Barry Seal
City Hall, Bradford
West Yorkshire BD1 1HY
Tel: 0274 726288
Fax: 0274 752065

Glasgow
Mrs Janey Buchan
Glasgow European
Constituency Office
38-40 New City Road
Cowcaddens
Glasgow G4 9JT
Tel: 041 353 3815
Fax: 041 353 2830

Highlands and Islands
Mrs Winifred Ewing
52 Queen's Drive
Glasgow G42 8DD
Tel: 041 423 1765
Fax: 041 422 1222

Lothian
Mr David Martin
15 Windsor Street
Edinburgh EH7 5LA
Tel: 031 557 0936
Fax: 031 557 5671

Mid Scotland and Fife
Mr Alexander Falconer
25 Church Street
Inverkeithing
Fife KY11 1LH
Tel: 0383 419330
Fax: 0383 419437

North East Scotland
Mr Henry McCubbin
58 Castle Street
Broughty Ferry
Dundee DD5 2EJ
Tel: 0382 730773
Fax: 0382 736858

South of Scotland
Mr Alex Smith
35 Kersland Foot
Girdle Toll
Irvine KA11 1BP
Tel: 0294 216704

Strathclyde East
Mr Kenneth Collins
11 Stuarton Park
East Kilbride G74 4LA
Tel: 0355 237282
Fax: 0355 249670

Strathclyde West
Mr Hugh McMahon
Abbey Mill Business
Centre
Seedhill Road
Paisley PA1 1JN
Tel: 041 889 9990
Fax: 041 889 4790

Mid and West Wales
Mr David Morris
39 St James Crescent
Swansea SA1 6DR
Tel: 0792 6435452
Fax: 0792 646430

North Wales
Mr Anthony Wilson
14 Post Office Lane
Denbigh
Clwyd LL16 3UN
Tel: 0745 814434
Fax: 0745 814434

South East Wales
Mr Llewellyn Smith
23 Beaufort Street
Brynmawr
Gwent NP3 4AQ
Tel: 0495 313345
Fax: 0495 313346

South Wales
Mr Wayne David
199 Newport Road
Cardiff CF2 1AJ
Tel: 0222 490215
Fax: 0222 487758

Northern Ireland
Mr John Hume
5 Bayview Terrace, Derry
Tel: 0504 265340

Mr James Nicholson
147 Keady Road
Ballyards
Armagh BT60 3AE
Tel: 0861 523307
Fax: 0861 523307

Rev. Ian Paisley
256 Ravenhill Road
Belfast BT6 8GJ
Tel: 0232 454255
Fax: 0232 457783

Which countries are in which organisation

European Community Member States

Belgium	Greece	Netherlands
Denmark	Ireland	Portugal
France	Italy	Spain
Germany	Luxembourg	United Kingdom

The following countries have formally applied for Membership of the European Community:

Austria	Malta	Turkey
Cyprus	Sweden	
Finland	Switzerland	

European Free Trade Area Member States

Austria	Liechtenstein	Switzerland
Finland	Norway	
Iceland	Sweden	

The **European Economic Area** comprises all the EFTA countries and all the European Community countries.

Additional Information on the European Community

Constitutional basis of the EC

There are three "Communities" that make up the EC. These are the European Coal and Steel Community, based on the Treaty of Paris of 1951, the European Atomic Energy Community and the European Economic Community, both based on treaties signed in Rome in 1957. The founding treaties have been amended from time to time, most notably by the "Single European Act" of 1986 and by the, still to be ratified, Maastricht Treaty of 1992.

Brussels EC headquarters

Until the end of 1991, all the Commissioners and their cabinets and some of the staff of the Commission worked in the "Berlaymont" – the building in the shape of a curved cross that often appeared on our television screens. Today that building stands empty while it is cleared of asbestos, though its address (200 rue de la Loi, 1049 Brussels) is still used for postal purposes. Most of the members of staff of the Commission are accommodated in the surrounding streets in some 25 different buildings.

Commission culture

Although in some ways the 17 person Commission, appointed every 4 years, acts like a government (for example it acts collegiately with each member having departmental responsibilities), it has none of the political cohesiveness that we expect in the government of the UK. Members come from widely differing cultural and political backgrounds and probably had very little contact with each other before the start of their four year term of office.

Subsidiarity

This is the principle that decisions are taken at the level appropriate to those who will be affected, be it local, regional, national or community level.

Additionality

This is the principle of the co-funding of projects by the EC Structural Funds and Member States, frequently on a 50:50 basis, thereby implying that EC funding is in addition to, and not a substitute for, national funding.

Appendix 5   **Flow Chart of Decision-Making in the European Community**

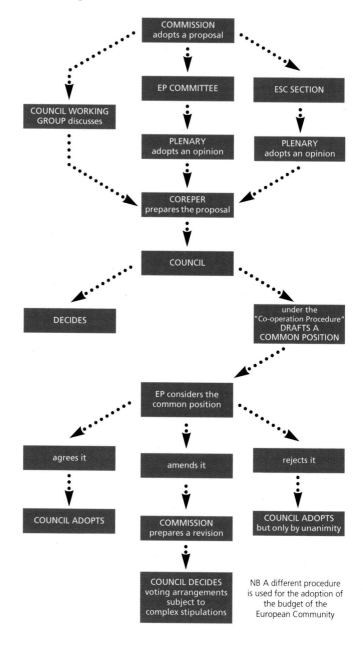

NB A different procedure is used for the adoption of the budget of the European Community

Directives, Regulations and other Community Procedural Terminology

A Regulation

A regulation is a law which applies directly throughout the Community. A regulation is used when the need for consistency across the Community is greater than the need to pay attention to the different national situations. Regulation 2052 of 24th June 1988, for example, establishes the broad outlines of the work of the Community's Structural Funds (see box page 39).

A Directive

A directive is a law which applies throughout the Community. However, it applies indirectly, by requiring that national legislation is introduced or amended to ensure that the provisions of the directive are brought into force in the various countries of the Community.

Directives are widely used. Their great advantage is that they allow common objectives to be secured with a minimum of disruption to existing legal arrangements.

The Directive of 21st December 1988 (89/48/EEC), for example, laid down the requirements for recognition throughout the Community of higher education diplomas involving at least three years' study. It came into effect on 4th January 1989 and countries had two years from that date to comply with its requirements and inform the Commission that they had done so. In fact rather few countries achieved this target but their failure did not necessarily deprive Community nationals from their rights under the directive, though it made claiming them more complicated.

A Decision

A decision by the Council is legally binding, but only on specified parties such as Community countries, companies or individuals. Decisions can be used to establish EC programmes. For example, the Council Decision 88/231 of 18th April 1988 provided the legal basis for the HELIOS programme in favour of people with disabilities.

Resolutions, Recommendations, Opinions, Conclusions

These acts of the Council have no legal force. They reflect and help to shape public policy in the subjects covered.

Under certain circumstances the Commission can itself enact forms of legislation, rather as the UK government can frame statutory instruments. It issues many regulations, for example, in the course of managing the Common Agricultural Policy. It uses decisions notably in ensuring that competition and free movement are not restrained. Thus in Decision 92/261 of 18th March 1992, the Commission found that Dunlop Slazenger International Ltd, with others, had infringed an article of the Treaty of Rome in the way in which tennis balls had been marketed in the Netherlands. The decision also fined the firms concerned. Decisions like this can be the subject of an appeal to the Court of Justice. Indeed Dunlop Slazenger have made such an appeal in this case on the grounds that the Commission was wrong in procedure, inference and law.

Appendix 7

Useful Contacts

EC Ministers responsible for sport

Mr Bernard ANSELME
(French Community)
Ministre-Président de la
Communauté
Française Chargé de la
Culture
19 A/D Avenue des Arts
1040 Brussels
BELGIUM
Tel: 010 (32) 2 220 55 11
Fax: 010 (32) 2 218 45 99

Mr Hugo WECKX
(Flemish Community)
Gemeenschapsminister
van Cultuur
Kunstlaan 46 (5e Verd)
1040 Brussels
BELGIUM
Tel: 010 (32) 2 513 91 59

Mr Joseph MARAITE
(German Community)
Gemeinschaftsminister
für Sport
Klötzerbahn 32
4700 Eupen
BELGIUM
Tel: 010 (32) 87 74 40 75

Mrs Grethe F ROSTBØLL
Minister For Culture
2 Nybrogade
1203 Copenhagen
DENMARK
Tel: 010 (45) 33 92 33 70
Fax: 010 (45) 33 91 33 88

Mme Frédérique BREDIN
Ministre de la Jeunesse et
des Sports
78 rue Olivier-de-Serres
75739 Paris
FRANCE CEDEX 15
Tel: 010 (33) 1 40 45 90 00
Fax: 010 (33) 1 48 28 91 49

Dr Rudolph SEITERS
Bundesminister des
Innern
Graurheindorferstr. 198
5300 Bonn 1
GERMANY
Tel: 010 (49) 228 681 1
Fax: 010 (49) 228 681 4665

Mr Vassilis
PAPAGEORGOPOULOS
Under Secretary of State
Ministry of Culture
General Secretariat for
Sports
Panepistimiou 25
PB 1013
10110 Athens
GREECE
Tel: 010 (30) 1 324 9500
Fax: 010 (30) 1 323 5011

Mr Liam AYLWARD TD
Minister of State
Ministry of Education
Marlborough Street
Dublin 1
IRELAND

Dr Carlo TOGNOLI
Ministry of Tourism and
Events
Via Della Ferratella 51
00184 Rome
ITALY
Tel: 010 (39) 6 7001 992
Fax: 010 (39) 6 7003 746

Mr Johny LAHURE
Ministre de l'Education
Physique
BP 180
2011 Luxembourg
LUXEMBOURG
Tel: 010 (352) 40 80 1
Fax: 010 (352) 43 45 99

Mrs Hedy d'ANCONA
Minister of Welfare
Health & Cultural Affairs
Sir Winston Churchill
Laan 366, PO Box 3007
2280 Mj Rijswijk
NETHERLANDS
Tel: 010 (31) 7340 7911

Mr A COUTO DOS
SANTOS
Minister for Education
Education Ministry
Avenida 5 De Outubro 107,
1000 Lisbon
PORTUGAL

Mr Javier SOLANA
MADARIAGA
Minister of Education
Consejo Superior de
Deportes
c/Martin Fierro s/n
28040 Madrid
SPAIN
Tel: 010 (34) 1 589 67 00
Fax: 010 (34) 1 544 39 94

Heads of Government Sports Departments

Mr Armand LAMS
(Flemish Community)
Directeur-Generaal
Ministerie van de
Vlaamse Gemeenschap
Gemeenschapsattaché
Koloniënstraat 31
1000 Brussels
BELGIUM
Tel: 010 (32) 2 510 34 45
Fax: 010 (32) 2 511 31 52

Mr Louis AWOUST
(French Community)
Director General for
Sport and Tourism
Ministry of Culture and
Social Affairs
44 Boulevard Léopold II
1080 Brussels
BELGIUM
Tel: 010 (32) 2 413 23 11
Fax: 010 (32) 2 413 28 25

Mr Leonhard SCHIFFLERS
(German Community)
Conseiller Sport
Minister for Sport
Klotzerbahn 32
4700 Eupen
BELGIUM

Mr Jorgen RASMUSSEN
Director General
Ministry of Cultural
Affairs
2 Nybrogade
1203 Copenhagen
DENMARK
Tel: 010 (45) 33 92 33 70
Fax: 010 (45) 33 91 33 88

Mr Philippe GRAILLOT
Directeur des Sports
Ministère de la Jeunesse
et des Sports
78 rue Olivier-de-Serres
75739 Paris
FRANCE CEDEX 15
Tel: 010(33) 1 40 45 90 00
Fax: 010(33)1 48 28 91 49

Mr Erich SCHAIBLE
Ministerialdirektor
Bundesministerium des
Innern
Graurheindorferstr. 198
5300 Bonn 1
GERMANY
Tel: 010(49)228 681 3590
Fax: 010(49)228 681 5515

Mr Kiriakos VIRVIDAKIS
Secretary General
General Secretariat for
Sport
Panepistimiou 25
10110 Athens
GREECE
Tel: 010 (30) 1 323 8852

Mr Con HAUGH
Principal Sports Officer
Department of Education
11th Floor
Hawkins House
Hawkins Street
Dublin 2
IRELAND
Tel: 010 (353) 1 73 47 00
Fax: 010 (353) 1 72 95 53

Mr Stefano Luigi TORDA
Director
Ministry of Tourism and
Events
Via della Ferratella 51
00184 Rome
ITALY
Tel: 010 (39) 6 7001 992
Fax: 010 (39) 6 7003 746

Mr Georges LANNERS
Director General for
Sport
Ministry of Physical
Education and Sport
BP 180
2011 Luxembourg
LUXEMBOURG
Tel: 010 (352) 43 10 14
Fax: 010 (352) 43 45 99

Mr Wim WAGEMAKER
Director of the Sports
Department
Ministry of Welfare,
Health and Cultural
Affairs
PO Box 3007
2280 Mj Rijswijk
NETHERLANDS
Tel: 010 (31) 7 340 6400
Fax: 010 (31) 7 340 6318

Mr Arcelino MIRANDELA
DA COSTA
Director Geral Dos
Desportos
Ave Infante Santo 76-4
1399 Lisbon CODEX
PORTUGAL
Tel: 010(351) 1 395 32 71
Fax: 010 (351) 1 60 26 04

Mr Rafael CORTES
ELVIRA
Director General
Consejo Superior de
Deportes
c/Martin Fierro s/n
28040 Madrid
SPAIN
Tel: 010 (34) 1 589 67 00
Fax: 010 (34) 1 544 39 94

**Government
Officers
responsible for
International
Affairs**

Mr Odon MARNEFFE
(French Community)
Ministry of Culture and
Social Affairs
44 Boulevard Léopold II
1080 Brussels
BELGIUM
Tel: 010 (32) 2 413 23 11
Fax: 010 (32) 2 413 28 25

Mr André VAN LIERDE
(Flemish Community)
BLOSO
Koloniënstraat 31
1000 Brussels
BELGIUM
Tel: 010 (32) 2 512 09 66
Fax: 010 (32) 2 512 88 63

Mr Claus Lützau FORUP
Head of Section
Ministry of Culture
2 Nybrogade
1203 Copenhagen
DENMARK
Tel: 010 (45) 33 92 33 70
Fax: 010 (45) 33 91 33 88

Mr Renaud NATTIEZ
Head of International
Sports Affairs
Ministère de la Jeunesse
et des Sports
78 Rue Olivier-de-Serres
75739 Paris
FRANCE CEDEX 15
Tel: 010(33) 1 40 45 99 75
Fax: 010(33) 1 48 28 91 49

Mr Peter GLASS
Head of International
Sports Affairs
Bundesministerium des
Innern
Graurheindorferstr. 198
5300 Bonn 1
GERMANY
Tel: 010(49)228 681 46 81
Fax: 010(49)228 681 55 15

Ms Maria
PAPATHANASSIOU
Head of International
Relations Bureau
General Secretariat for
Sport
Panepistimiou 25
10110 Athens
GREECE
Tel: 010 (30) 1 323 88 62
Fax: 010 (30) 1 323 04 58

Mr Robert SCHULER
Head of International
Sports Affairs
Ministry of Physical
Education and Sport
BP 180
2011 Luxembourg
LUXEMBOURG
Tel: 010 (352) 43 10 14
Fax: 010 (352) 43 45 99

Mr Ronald KRAMER
Division Manager
Sports Department
Ministry of Welfare,
Health and Cultural
Affairs
PO Box 3007
2280 Mj Rijswijk
NETHERLANDS
Tel: 010 (31) 7 340 6393
Fax: 010 (31) 7 340 6318

Mr Manuel BOA DE
JESUS
Head of International
Relations
Direcçao Geral dos
Desportos
Ave Infante Santo 76-2
1399 Lisbon CODEX
PORTUGAL
Tel: 010 (351) 1 397 79 36
Fax: 010 (351) 1 60 26 04

Mrs Ana Cristina
GOZALO AUSIN
International Relations
Consejo Superior de
Deportes
c/Martin Fierro s/n
28040 Madrid
SPAIN
Tel: 010 (34) 1 589 66 29
Fax: 010 (34) 1 544 39 94

**Non-Governmental
Organisations**

Mr Adrian VAN DEN
EEDE
Belgian Olympic &
Interféderal Committee
Avenue de Bouchout 9
1020 Brussels
BELGIUM
Tel: 010 (32) 2 479 1940
Fax: 010 (32) 2 479 4656

Mr Bent AGERSKOV
Secretary General
The Danish Sports
Federation
Idraettens Hus
Brøndby Stadion 20
2605 Brøndby
DENMARK
Tel: 010 (45) 42 45 41 76
Fax: 010 (45) 42 45 62 45

Mr Maurice PELUCHON
Directeur, Départment
Sport de Masse et de la
Formation
23, rue d'Anjou
75008 Paris
FRANCE
Tel: 010 (33) 1 42 65 02 74
Fax: 010 (33) 1 42 68 12 98

Mrs Marlis RYDZY-GÖTZ
Head of International
Relations
Deutscher Sportbund
Otto-Fleck-Schneise 12
6000 Frankfurt 71
GERMANY
Tel: 010 (49) 069 67 00 217
Fax: 010 (49) 069 67 49 06

Mr Eamonn DOHERTY
Sport For All Committee
(COSPOIR)
National Sports Council
51 Pinewood Park
Rathfarnham
Dublin 14
IRELAND
Tel: 010 (353) 1 93 47 95
Fax: 010 (353) 1 72 95 53

Mr Mario PESCANTE
Secretary General
Comitato Olympico
Nazionale Italiano
Foro Italico
00194 Rome
ITALY
Tel: 010 (39) 6 321 9751
Fax: 010 (39) 6 322 7970

Mr Emile THOMA
Secretary General
Comité Olympique et
Sportif
7 Avenue Victor Hugo
1750 Luxembourg
LUXEMBOURG
Tel: 010 (352) 47 13 47

Mr Wim de HEER
Secretary General
Netherlands Sport
Federation
PO Box 302
6800 Arnhem
NETHERLANDS
Tel: 010 (31) 8 308 34 400
Fax: 010 (31) 8 308 21 245

**Association of
European National
Olympic
Committees
(AENOC)**

Dr Jacques ROGGE
Comité Olympique et
Interfederal Belge
Avenue De Bouchout 9
1020 Brussels
BELGIUM
Tel: 010 (32) 2 479 1940
Fax: 010 (32) 2 478 9673

European Non-Governmental Sports Organisation (ENGSO)

Mr Norbert WOLF
ENGSO Chairman
c/o Deutscher Sportbund
Otto-Fleck-Schneise 12
6000 Frankfurt 71
GERMANY
Tel:010(49)069 67 00 217
Fax: 010 (49) 069 67 49 06

Mr Stig HEDLUND
ENGSO Secretary
c/o Swedish Sports
Confederation
Idrottens Hus
12387 Farsta
SWEDEN
Tel: 010 (46) 8 605 6000
Fax: 010 (46) 8 605 6200

Council of Europe Clearing House

Mr Albert REMANS
Executive Director
Clearing House
Espace du 27 Septembre
4e étage, Boulevard
Léopold II, 44
1080 Brussels
BELGIUM
Tel: 010 (32) 2 413 2893
Fax: 010 (32) 2 413 2890

Council of Europe CDDS Secretariat

Mr George WALKER
Head of Sports Division
Council of Europe
Directorate of Education,
Culture & Sport
BP 431 R6
67006 Strasbourg
FRANCE
Tel: 010 (33) 88 41 20 00
Fax: 010 (33) 88 41 27 88

General Association of International Sports Federations (GAISF)

Mr Luc NIGGLI
Secretary General
Villa Henri
7 Boulevard de Suisse
98000 Monaco
Tel: 010 (33) 93 50 74 13
Fax: 010 (33) 93 25 28 73

Permanent Representation of the UK to the European Communities

HE Sir John KERR KCMG
Rond Point Robert
Schuman 6
1040 Brussels
BELGIUM
Tel: 010 (32) 287 82 11
Fax: 010 (32) 287 83 98

UK Addresses

Sports Minister

Mr Robert KEY
Minister with
Responsibility for Sport
Department of National
Heritage
Sanctuary Buildings
Great Smith Street
LONDON
SW1P 3BT

Department of National Heritage

Miss A J STEWART
Head of Sport and
Recreation Division
and
Mr Neville MACKAY
Responsible for
International Affairs
Department of National
Heritage
Sanctuary Buildings
Great Smith Street
LONDON
SW1P 3BT
Tel: 010 (44) 71 925 6370
Fax: 010 (44) 71 925 6394

Sports Council

Mr David PICKUP
Director General
and
Mr Derek CASEY
Deputy Director General
The Sports Council
16 Upper Woburn Place
LONDON
WC1H 0QP
Tel: 010 (44) 71 388 1277
Fax: 010 (44) 71 388 5470

Mr Iain REDDISH
Head of International
Affairs
The Sports Council
Walkden House
3-10 Melton Street
LONDON
NW1 2EB
Tel: 010 (44) 71 383 3896
Fax: 010 (44) 71 383 3147

Mr Linford TATHAM
Director
Sports Council for Wales
Sophia Gardens
CARDIFF
CF1 9SW
Tel: 010 (44) 222 397571
Fax: 010 (44) 222 222431

Mr Allan ALSTEAD
Chief Executive
Scottish Sports Council
Caledonia House
South Gyle
EDINBURGH
EH12 9DQ
Tel: 010 (44) 31 317 7200
Fax: 010 (44) 31 317 7202

Mr J E MILLER
Director
Sports Council for
Northern Ireland
House of Sport
Upper Malone Road
BELFAST
BT9 5LA
Tel: 010 (44) 232 381222
Fax: 010 (44) 232 682757

Non-Governmental Organisations

Mr Alan GROSSET
Secretary
British Sports Forum
c/o Alex Morrison & Co
33 Queens Street
EDINBURGH
EH2 1LE
Tel: 010 (44) 31 226 6541
Fax: 010 (44) 31 226 3156

Mr Dick PALMER
Secretary General
British Olympic
Association*
1 Wandsworth Plain
LONDON
SW18 1EH
Tel: 010 (44) 81 871 2677
Fax: 010 (44) 81 871 9104

Mr Peter LAWSON
Secretary General
Central Council of
Physical Recreation*
Francis House
Francis Street
LONDON
SW1P 1DE
Tel: 010 (44) 71 828 3163
Fax: 010 (44) 71 630 8820

Mr Fred NELSON
Chairman
and
Mr Terry DOWEY
General Secretary
Scottish Sports
Association*
Caledonia House
South Gyle
EDINBURGH
EH12 9DQ
Tel: 010 (44) 31 339 8785
Fax: 010 (44) 31 317 7202

Ms Joan McCLOY
Chairman
and
Mr George GLASGOW
Secretary
Northern Ireland Council
of Physical Recreation*
House of Sport
Upper Malone Road
BELFAST
BT9 5LA
Tel: 010 (44) 232 381222
Fax: 010 (44) 232 682757

Ms Wendy WILLIAMS
Chairman
and
Mr Graham DAVIES
Secretary
Welsh Sports
Association*
Sophia Gardens
CARDIFF
CF1 9SW
Tel: 010 (44) 222 397571
Fax: 010 (44) 222 222431

* Organisations in
  membership of
  the British Sports Forum

Council of Europe Member States   Appendix 8

Austria	Hungary	Portugal
Belgium	Iceland	San Marino
Bulgaria	Ireland	Spain
Cyprus	Italy	Sweden
Czechoslovakia	Liechtenstein	Switzerland
Denmark	Luxembourg	Turkey
Finland	Malta	United Kingdom
France	Netherlands	
Germany	Norway	
Greece	Poland	

Non-Member States which are contracting parties to the European Cultural Convention and therefore Members of the CDDS

Albania	Latvia	Russia
Estonia	Lithuania	Slovenia
The Holy See	Rumania	

Index

© The Sports Council
16 Upper Woburn Place
London WC1H 0QP
SC/129/3M/12/92
ISBN 1872158 110

The Sports Council was incorporated by Royal Charter in 1972 and its main objectives are to increase participation in sport and physical recreation, to increase the quantity and quality of sports facilities, to raise standards of performance and to provide information for and about sport.

Design by Wylie Design Company, London.
Printed in England by Ancient House Press, Ipswich.